JAY SCHMIDT

FORT WARREN
NEW ENGLAND'S MOST HISTORIC CIVIL WAR SITE

Jay Schmidt

UBT
PRESS

Published by UBT Press, Amherst, NH 03031

Cover design by Renee Sartell
Front cover photo by Jay Schmidt
Back cover photo by Ryan Vines
Author photo by Jennifer Schmidt

Printed in the United States of America by King Printing Co.

10   9   8   7   6   5   4   3   2   1

ISBN 0-9721489-4-9

First Edition 2003

Fort Warren has more memories of the Civil War days than any other place in New England.

Edward Rowe Snow
1902-1982

Photo courtesy of Dorothy Snow Bicknell

CONTENTS

INTRODUCTION

Fort Warren served as one of the main defenders of Boston Harbor for four wars. This heavily fortified granite fort was built on a remote island before the Civil War to protect the main shipping channels. It was additionally used to train Union troops and served as a prison for captured Confederates. During the Spanish-American War, Fort Warren's garrison protected the citizens of Boston.

Throughout the years there have been major modifications to the fort to accomodate the addition of current weapons. The fort continued to serve major defense roles in both World Wars I and II. Modern weapons (aircraft and nuclear weapons), however, finally rendered the fort obsolete for military purposes shortly after World War II. In the late 1950s, the fort was transferred to the Metropolitan District Commission (MDC) for recreational use. Today it is open to the public as the centerpiece of the Boston Harbor Islands, National Park Area.

In the mid 1950s I had the privilege of touring the decommissioned fort while it was still under federal control and off-limits to visitors. My friend's father was a pilot on one of the Boston fireboats. On Sundays the fireboats were allowed to take families and friends along for routine harbor inspections. We went to Fort Warren for a fire inspection, and we got a guided tour of the fort by the resident caretaker. I was too young, unfortunately, to realize its historical significance.

Later I received some of Edward Rowe Snow's nautical books as gifts (he was my father's history teacher, and my mother's math teacher at Winthrop, Mass., High School.) Because of his sea stories, I developed a profound interest in the fort. I wanted to pick up where Edward Rowe Snow left off and tell more of the story of Fort Warren.

I wrote this book primarily for those who have an interest in Civil War history, and for the many thousands of visitors who tour the fort each summer.

Some of the information had conflicting names and dates (even by the same source). In every case, I have tried to get the most accurate information possible.

This book answers the question, "What went on at Fort Warren?"

Jay Schmidt
Norton, Mass.

ACKNOWLEDGMENTS

I would like to thank the following people who gave me editorial support and valuable information which helped make this book possible: Jim Fahey, Jeremy D'Entremont, Gerald W. Butler, Edmund "Duke" MacNeil, Tom Vaughan, Scott Salesses, Paul Lawton, Martha Rice and Dorothy Snow Bicknell (Edward Rowe Snow's daughter) who graciously granted permission for me to use some of her father's material. She also gave me access to his personal Fort Warren photo collection. I also wish to thank multiple award-winning book cover designer Renee Sartell for her excellent cover design.

The Metropolitan District Commission (MDC) provided me with material from their Fort Warren files. I would especially like to thank Tom Bender and Bill Stokinger of the MDC for their help with this book. Bill volunteered his time not only to check (and correct) my final draft for accuracy, but he also added substantial historical information from his personal Fort Warren files.

I want to thank my wife Donna who was my proofreader and my chief cheerleader, and also my father Jim Schmidt for providing some of the illustrations.

Fort Warren

1

THE GHOST
OF THE
LADY IN BLACK

E very Boy Scout camp has its legends and resident ghost stories
that are told around every campfire. Many Boston islands and
lighthouses also have stories about ghosts and supernatural hap-
penings, but perhaps the most famous ghost story of them all is
the Lady in Black at Fort Warren.

Historian Edward Rowe Snow loved to tell this story. In fact,
he would take visitors on tours at Fort Warren and would tap on
a wooden door which opened up and a "ghost" (one of his asso-
ciates in a black dress) would pop out of a hole dug in the ground
and frighten everyone at a key moment of the tale.

No one tells the story better, so here is the Edward Rowe
Snow version—reprinted with permission from his family.

> The legend of the famous Lady in Black has been whis-
> pered at Fort Warren for many, many years, until now
> there are quite a few who believe in the existence of
> this lady of black robes. I herewith offer the legend
> without the slightest guarantee that any part of it is true.
>
> During the War between the States, hundreds of pris-
> oners were captured by Burnside at Roanoke Island.
> Among the group incarcerated at Fort Warren in the
> Corridor of Dungeons was a young lieutenant who had
> been married only a few weeks before. He succeeded
> in getting a message to his young wife by the under-
> ground railroad, giving complete directions as to where
> he was and how she could reach him.
>
> Being very much in love, she obtained passage on a
> small sloop, and landed in Hull a few weeks later. She

1

quickly located the home of a Southerner in that town and was fitted out with a pistol and dressed in men's clothing.

Choosing a dark, rainy night, the lady rowed across Nantasket Road [a shipping anchorage] and finally landed on the beach at George's Island. Slipping noiselessly by the sentries, she reached the ditch under the Corridor of Dungeons. After giving a prearranged signal, she was hoisted up to the carronade embrasure and pulled through the opening.

As soon as husband and wife had exchanged greetings, they made plans for the future. The prisoners decided to dig their way out of the dungeon into the parade ground and set to work. Unfortunately for their plans, a slight miscalculation brought their tunnel within hearing of Northern soldiers stationed on the other side of the wall. The commanding officer, Colonel Dimick was notified and the whole scheme was quickly exposed.

The brave little woman, when cornered, attempted to fire at the Colonel, but the gun was of the old fashioned pepper box type and exploded, killing her husband.

Colonel Dimick had no alternative but to sentence her to hang as a spy. She made one last request: that she be hanged in women's clothing. After a search of the fort, some robes were found which had been worn by one of the soldiers during an entertainment, and the plucky girl went to her death wearing these robes.

At various times through the years, the Ghost of the Lady in Black has returned to haunt the men quartered at the fort. Once three soldiers were walking under the great arched sally port at the entrance to the fort, and there before them, in the fresh snow, were five impressions of a girl's shoe leading nowhere and coming from nowhere. In 1934, a certain sergeant from Fort Banks was climbing to the top of the ladder which leads to the Corridor of Dungeons when he heard a voice warning him, saying: "Don't come in here!" Needless to say, he did not venture further.

There actually are on record court-martial cases of men who have shot at ghost-like figures while on sentry duty, and one poor man deserted his post, claiming he had been chased by the lady of the black robes.

For many years the traditional poker game was enjoyed in the old ordnance storeroom, and at ten o'clock one night a stone was rolled the entire length

The Ghost of the Lady in Black is said to still haunt Fort Warren.
Illustration by Jim Schmidt

of the storeroom. As all the men on the island were playing poker, no explanation could be found. When the same thing happened the next time that the men played poker in the evening, the group at the card table decreased appreciably.

By the end of the month the ordnance storeroom was deserted, and since that time, if any of the enlisted men wished to indulge in this pastime, they chose another part of the island. The ghost of the "Lady in Black" was, of course, blamed for the trouble.

Excerpted from *The Romance of Boston Bay.*

Is the story about the Lady in Black true? Probably not. It is a thrilling legend which has spanned many generations of Fort Warren soldiers. The coast artillery soldiers stationed at Fort Warren

Historian Edward Rowe Snow tells the tale of the Lady in Black in the Corridor of Dungeons at Fort Warren.
Photo courtesy of Dorothy Snow Bicknell

in World War II would taunt one another when it was time for guard duty. They would yell, "Watch out for the Black Widow!" to the soldiers heading out onto the lonely grounds at night.

Although many people believe this story was based on fact, I did not find any stories in the Boston newspapers at that time about a woman's hanging. There were regular newspaper correspondence from Fort Warren by reporters who visited the fort, but no story about a woman being hanged as a spy. This would have been a tremendous story.

The only known woman executed during the Civil War era was Mary Surratt, one of the conspirators in the Lincoln assassination.

Could it be true after all, and no one retained accurate records of it? Possibly, but not likely. Most of Fort Warren's official records were destroyed by a low-level bureaucrat after the fort was decommissioned following World War II.

Ghost stories from the fort continued. Gerald Butler, a former curator (1971–72) at Fort Warren lived at the fort in the early 1970s for about a year. One night he was up in Bastion B replacing a window in the observation tower about 10 P.M., on a chilly, windless winter evening. He heard the distinctive clicking sounds of footsteps coming towards him along the ramparts. "It was unnerving and made my hair stand up," said Butler. Other than his wife and daughter who were asleep in the house, there was not a soul on the island.

Butler recalled another strange Fort Warren incident. MDC Police details were assigned in the late 1960s to protect the fort from vandalism and theft. One officer's dog was afraid to go into Bastion A. "The dog would go anywhere on the fort, but once it got to Bastion A, the dog would *always* refuse to go inside," said Butler.

About 1981, a group of Civil War reenactors slept in the fort during a reenactment weekend. They were on the parade grounds in their tents during a rainstorm. One of the reenactors, at about 3 A.M., looked out of his tent to check the weather. He saw what appeared to be a lantern on the parapets moving with nobody holding it. The reenactors also observed a dark figure, and they found it difficult to go back to sleep after this experience.

Scientists became involved in the Black Widow legend. During the mid-1970s technicians and scientists reportedly from MIT (the Massachusetts Institute of Technology) were attempting to record on special film ectoplasmic apparitions tying in with telekinesis and other spiritual media. Since Fort Warren had numerous spiritual sightings and other phenomena, they went to the fort.

The group set up cameras at various locations during this unofficial study. Later, one or two frames showed a ghostly apparition of the famous Black Widow at the Scarp Gallery of the fort.

Former Fort Warren curator Gerald Butler has seen the pictures. "It did *look* as if there was a woman apparition facing the camera with a sun bonnet and shawl," he recalled. The explanation? Butler had none. "It could have been air currents, or a fog or something. It could have been a mild hoax for inter-office chuckles at MIT," he added.

Then again, it could have been the Lady in Black.

2

EARLY HISTORY

George's Island in Boston Harbor was first called Pemberton's Island after James Pemberton who lived there in the early 1600s.

Pemberton's Island was later called George's Island after John George, who lived on the island by the 1680s. Incidentally, the apostrophe is sometimes dropped. The National Park Service doesn't use the apostrophe on any of its signage, but the Metropolitan District Commission (MDC), which controls the island, still uses the apostrophe. Either spelling is considered correct. For the purpose of consistency, I kept the apostrophe in this book to match the MDC.

The Narrows as seen today from George's Island. It was once the main shipping channel into Boston. Lovell's Island is in the background.
Photo by Jay Schmidt

Previously, only colonial earthen fortifications stood on the island when it was used by French troops during the Revolution. In 1711, it was a place for Sir Hovendon Walker's sick British soldiers and sailors to recuperate.

During the War of 1812, a famous naval battle occurred several miles from George's Island. The British frigate HMS *Shannon* mounting 52 guns, commanded by Captain Philip Broke was blockading Boston Harbor. He sent a letter to Captain James Lawrence of the 49-gun American frigate USS *Chesapeake,* anchored in Boston Harbor, challenging him to a ship-to-ship battle. On June 1, 1813, the Chesapeake left her anchorage in President Roads and sailed out past George's Island to confront the *Shannon* which was patrolling between Cape Ann and Cape Cod.

About 5:30 P.M., approximately 21 miles from Boston Light, the two ships engaged in a furious battle. In less than 15 minutes, the battle was over. The *Chesapeake* had been boarded and

The USS Chesapeake *(left) approaching the HMS* Shannon *about 21–23 miles from Georges Island during their famous battle of 1813.*
Library of Congress

defeated with the loss of 48 killed and 98 wounded. During the battle, the mortally wounded Captain Lawrence uttered the famous words, "Don't give up the ship!"

The *Chesapeake*, however, was captured and later served in the Royal Navy as a war prize. A few months later, Captain Oliver Hazard Perry flying a blue banner with Lawrence's words, "Don't give up the ship" defeated the British Navy during the Battle of Lake Erie. The slogan, which was made famous by Captain Perry, became a favorite phrase of the U.S. Navy.

Army engineers had determined that George's Island had a commanding position right between the main shipping channels, and permanent anchorage, leading into Boston at that time. Enemy ships could not enter Boston Harbor without passing directly by the island. It was the perfect island on which to build a fort.

Fort Warren was built, of course, to protect Boston from an attack by enemy ships. On March 3, 1833 construction began on the island. The five-sided, pentagonal-shaped granite fort's

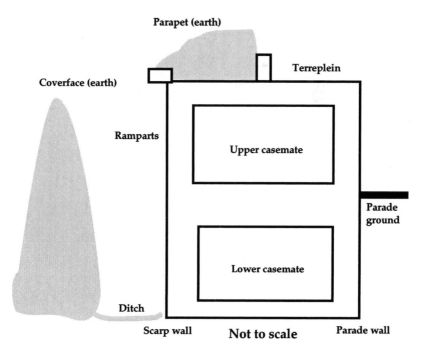

A cross section of Fort Warren showing the various nomenclature.
Illustration by Jay Schmidt

construction was supervised by Colonel Sylvanus Thayer, of Braintree, Mass., who was previously superintendent of West Point. While still under construction, the fort was named Fort Warren after Dr. Joseph Warren who was killed at the nearby Battle of Bunker Hill during the Revolutionary War on June 17, 1775. An original portrait of Dr. Warren still hangs today in the home of President John Adams in the Adams National Historical

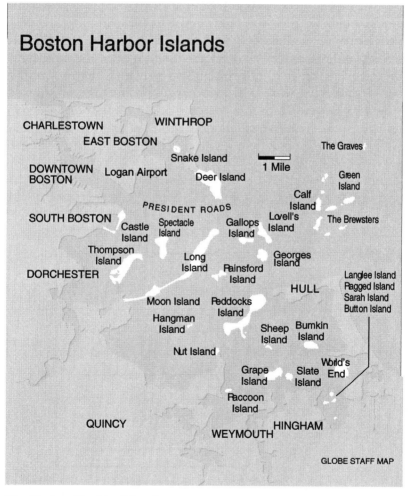

Boston Harbor Islands

CHARLESTOWN
WINTHROP
EAST BOSTON
The Graves
Snake Island
1 Mile
DOWNTOWN BOSTON
Logan Airport
Deer Island
Green Island
Calf Island
PRESIDENT ROADS
SOUTH BOSTON
Lovell's Island
The Brewsters
Castle Island
Spectacle Island
Gallops Island
Thompson Island
Long Island
Georges Island
DORCHESTER
Rainsford Island
Langlee Island
Ragged Island
Sarah Island
Button Island
HULL
Moon Island
Peddocks Island
Hangman Island
Sheep Island
Bumkin Island
Nut Island
World's End
Grape Island
Slate Island
Raccoon Island
QUINCY
HINGHAM
WEYMOUTH

GLOBE STAFF MAP

The Boston Harbor Islands.
Reprinted courtesy of the *Boston Globe*

Park in Quincy, Mass. The fort was originally designed to hold about 300 cannon. It was known as one of the strongest coastal fortifications ever built in the United States.

Granite from both Cape Ann and nearby Quincy, Mass., was used in the construction of the fort which was still somewhat unfinished at the start of the Civil War. Upon early inspection, military commanders were not satisfied with the armaments at the fort. When the governor visited after the start of the war, they had to struggle to find enough powder to render a single gun salute. Even when the first troops arrived, the fort was still not yet ready for occupancy. The Second Batallion of Infantry (called the Tigers) from Boston arrived on April 29, 1861 and had to clean up the parade ground and living quarters.

The *Harper's Weekly* Dec. 7, 1861 issue published an excellent description of the fort.

Here are some excerpts.

> The general plan of the fortification is a figure of five sides or fronts, with bastions, curtains, flanks and faces. The top of the parapet is 70 feet above low-water mark, while the heights of the parade wall is 25 feet, and that of the scarp or exterior wall 30 feet. The main fort is entirely surrounded by a ditch of 30 feet wide . . . The terreplein, upon which is to be planted with barbette guns, is 27 feet wide, and extends entirely around the top of the fort. The pintles and traverse stones or circles upon which the guns are to be worked, have been set on the most commanding fronts, but at the present time only one gun, and that a Columbiad, in the casemates, is mounted. Measures have, however, been taken to supply the fort with a battery of rifled cannon.
>
> . . . All vessels entering the harbor are obliged to pass between "Bug Light" and the fort, and within half a mile of this formidable battery . . . The northeasterly front, commanding the Narrows, mounts 32 barbette [platform] guns on the terre-plein and 47 on a cover-face, which extends the entire length of the front. The battery on the northwesterly front, also commanding the Narrows, will consist of 35 barbette guns, and several flank guns for defending the ditches and main entrance to the port.

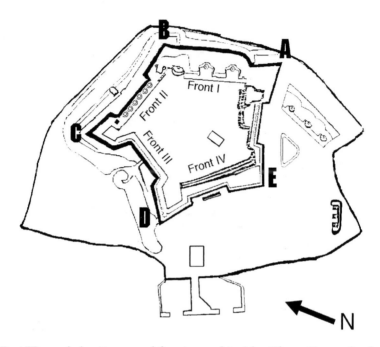

Fort Warren's bastions and fronts used to identify sections of a fort.
Illustration by Jay Schmidt based on an MDC map

. . . The main guardhouse is at the entrance of the ditch, on the left flank of this front. It consists of two square rooms, built of solid masonry, under the embankment, and well warmed and lighted.

. . . The quarters of the officers of the garrison are located in the casemates of the northwesterly front, which is pierced by the main entrance. There are eight sets of apartments, four of which, in the curtain, are finished with marble mantles and fire places, and plastered and painted in a style equal to first-class dwellings. Each set of quarters has a cistern of about twenty hogsheads' capacity.

. . . Some attempt has been made to ornament the grounds surrounding the fort by planting from 800 to 1000 shade trees. They are, however, quite young, and as yet do not afford much shade.

Captain Raphael Semmes (right) on the CSS Alabama. Some Bostonians feared an attack from this Confederate raider.
National Archives

   The people of Boston feared that the notorious Confederate raider Alabama could sail into the harbor and wreak havoc on the city and the ships tied up at the wharfs. It turned out that Captain Raphael Semmes and his CSS *Alabama*, being a commerce raider, never did attempt to enter Boston Harbor during the Civil War. (It is interesting to note that the Alabama's exploits were later used as a model for the German WWI U-boat tactics of sinking merchant ships. These same tactics were later copied by U.S. WWII submarines against the Japanese.)

The first Federal commander of Fort Warren, Colonel Justin E. Dimick, arrived from Fort Monroe in the fall of 1861. He was a venerable old soldier, and he was put out to pasture at Fort Warren to await retirement as the military prison's commander.

The first of the Massachusetts regiments trained at Fort Warren was the 12th Massachusetts (The Webster Regiment) commanded by Colonel Fletcher Webster—son of the famous statesman, Daniel Webster. Companies A and B entered the fort on May 1, 1861. Five companies were recruited from Boston and one company each came from East Abington, North Bridgewater, Gloucester, Stoughton and Weymouth. The 12th was mustered into U.S. service on June 26, and on July 23, they left Fort Warren and headed for the battlefields. Many of the Second Battalion Tigers enlisted in the 12th.

In June of 1861, the 14th Massachusetts Regiment (The Essex County Regiment) moved in. One soldier wrote:

> Our first night at the fort was one long to be remembered, no provisions had been made for us, and as we had neither blankets nor overcoats, we were obliged to take the cold stone floor for bed with nothing to cover us, the cold wind blowing through the embrasures from the ocean.

The infamous army bean soup was often the butt of jokes. Some Fort Warren soldiers once held a mock funeral for the single bean they claimed they found in their bean soup. One soldier of the 12th Massachusetts stirred a large pot of soup and started to take off his uniform. An officer asked him what he was doing, and he replied, "I am going to dive into that soup to see if I can find a bean."

Boston caterers (and sutlers) heard about the poor quality of food and were soon selling meals to soldiers stationed at the fort. Soldiers also were known to have dug clams for fresh clam chowder from the beaches surrounding the fort. This was considered a treat.

On Wednesdays and Sundays civilians were allowed to visit the soldiers at the fort. It is reported that on one day 2,000 visitors came to the fort.

With all the troops leaving for the front, Governor Andrews obtained permission from the secretary of war to detach the 24th

Massachusetts from Readville to become prison guards at the fort in 1861. Fresh recruits were soon replacing the volunteers. When some recruits from the Boston area arrived, no rations were ready and all they had was tea and bread. That night in their quarters, the undisciplined recruits began throwing loaves of bread at each other, and when Colonel Dimick walked into the area to find out what was going on, he was hit in the face by a loaf of bread. The guilty recruit was dragged outside and scolded by his commander.

The first company of what would become the First Battalion Massachusetts Heavy Artillery was authorized in February 1862. The First Battalion, as finally organized, would serve as the fort's primary garrison for the rest of the war, assisted by several short-term units overtime.

On October 6, 1863 a telegraph line connecting Boston with Fort Warren was completed, and the military sent the first message. There are no known records of any of the telegraph messages sent during the Civil War, but details of the proposed 1864 escape were telegraphed to Boston.

In 1882, a travel writer wrote:

> The great pentagonal fortress with its bastions at each angle is composed of casemated walls in which, and protected by enormous thicknesses of masonry and earth, burrow the barracks, hospital, magazine, storehouses, ice house, cook and mess rooms, cisterns and a battery of heavy guns facing the sea.
>
> Above the casemates are the ramparts sheltered by massive parapets and traverses and sustaining lines of 10 and 15 inch guns. The huge guns now mounted are not valued for their long range or penetrating power, but have a well known reputation for delivering an almost irresistible smashing fire, which at the short range of the ship channel would be extremely destructive, even to ironclads.

Fort Warren earned its place in history because of the many famous people who were imprisoned there during the Civil War. The Corps of Engineers did not intend for the fort to be used as a prison, but because of the narrow musket loopholes, strong granite walls, and its forbidding isolation, it served effectively as a prison with little modification.

It was 45 years between Fort Warren's initial proposal to its actual occupancy, and it was considered obsolete even before construction was finally completed. This all happened during a period of great technological changes.

3

CIVIL WAR GUARD DUTY

At the beginning of the Civil War, Fort Warren's primary mission was to defend Boston Harbor and to train Union recruits. In October 1861, however, the Federal Government began sending Confederate prisoners to Fort Warren, and the local units stationed there suddenly became 19th century correctional officers as well as soldiers.

Fort Warren had artillery units assigned to the garrison. Newly formed volunteers underwent a form of what is now called Basic Combat Training.

The main guardhouse on the left still stands today. The small wooden sentry box on the right no longer exists. A huge concrete mine control casemate was built adjacent to the guardhouse in the early 1900s.
National Archives

Companies of the 24th Massachusetts Regiment had the task to help transform the fort into a prison. One of the members of the 24th wrote about conditions at the fort:

> To some it was monotonous and uneventful, the abode itself black and dreary, so that they were not all sorry to receive orders, on the 7th of December to leave the fort and return to the camp at Readville. Of course, the work was not what men enlisting for active service expected, and to the officers a continued stay presented little promise of promotion. Then, too, the regiment was separated, and the accommodations at the fort were not what officers and men desired.

In 1863 there were 704 officers and men garrisoned at Fort Warren. Because of the continuous transferring of troops in and out of the fort during the war, there are no clear records indicating if the fort ever reached its maximum strength.

In 1863 Boston, along with other major cities, was hit with an anti-draft riot. Mobs rioted over the new draft laws, and Fort Warren had to send troops into Boston to help control the crowds.

The parade ground in March 1864. Bastion B is in the center. A single Rodman cannon and several rifled smoothbores are mounted on the ramparts.
National Archives

A 15-inch Rodman cannon photographed at Fort Warren about 1863. Note the huge cannonball being carried by the men in the center.
National Archives

The daily routine for about 35 guards was two-hour shifts followed by four hours rest in the guardhouse. According to Edward Rowe Snow, "The daily detail consisted of about 75 men, some of whom guarded the space where the prisoners were allowed to exercise. At retreat, the guards went inside the casemates."

A picket line extended around the outside walls of the fort. Union sentries were also posted at the sally port, the staircases and the guardhouse.

The Confederate prisoners and Union soldiers frequently jeered at one another. There are records of Union guards singing songs about hanging Jeff Davis (the *John Brown* song). Confederate prisoners retaliated by taunting the guards about the terrible Union defeat at the Battle of Bull Run.

In the winter, ice often formed on the parade grounds. One soldier allegedly was blown across the ice-covered field and was thrown into the granite walls by the infamous New England winter winds.

Rodman cannons are facing the sea. Front II is on the right, Bastion C is in the center of this post-war photo.
Boston Public Library

Fort Warren was not a pleasant place to be stationed in the winter. During the winter of 1861-62, The First Battalion, Infantry's Major Parker wrote:

> Such duty on a bleak island, exposed to the terrible cold and storms of a New England winter, was no pastime. Occasionally, some of the outposts would be untenable by reason of the dash of waves, and often inspection and relief of posts were effected with great difficulty because of the icy condition of the ground. In the most severe storms the guard replaced by patrols, each of two men, who walked the line, one patrol being dispatched every fifteen or twenty minutes.

Daily life was harsh for the soldiers at Fort Warren, but, then again, all soldiers during the Civil War lived under primitive conditions. According to Minor McLain's research, rations for Union troops at Fort Warren, at that time, consisted of fresh beef with potatoes three times a week, salt beef, pork or bacon three times a week and baked beans on Sunday. Each soldier also received tea substituted for coffee and 22 ounces of soft bread or 16 ounces of hardtack each day.

The soldiers entertained themselves by playing musical instruments and outdoor games such as football when the weather cooperated. Troops were allowed to swim in the ocean and to catch fish and lobsters when off duty. The troops could also buy food from Boston caterers or the post sutler if they could afford the prices.

Mail was delivered daily to the soldiers, unless weather conditions prevented the steamer *May Queen* from making the trip from Boston. Citizens of the Boston area often sent the soldiers gift packages which contained useful items such as food, socks, tobacco, and pillows to help make them more comfortable while serving their country.

Soldiers pose for a photograph in front of a 15" Rodman at Fort Warren.
Boston Public Library

One of the common punishments at the time for any Union soldier caught violating the rules was the infamous log duty. The guilty soldier had to carry a large log from one bastion to another and throw it onto the log pile. He then picked up another log of equal size and carried it back to the first bastion and threw it onto the original pile of logs. This monotonous punishment cured many soldiers from breaking any of Fort Warren's strict military rules again.

4

THE JOHN BROWN SONG

Civil War soldiers often sang songs while on the march and when in camp. One of the most well-known marching songs of that conflict—that was known and sung by nearly all Union soldiers—was the *John Brown* song. Most people (including many historians) are unaware that the lyrics to the song were written at Fort Warren, and it was *not* completely about the famous abolitionist John Brown. The *John Brown* song was also about a Union soldier named John Brown.

On April 29, 1861, the Second Battalion of Infantry, known as the Boston Light Infantry (popularly called the *Tigers*) was sent

VOL. V.—No. 258.] NEW YORK, SATURDAY, DECEMBER 7, 1861. [SINGLE COPIES SIX CENTS. $2 50 PER YEAR IN ADVANCE.

Entered according to Act of Congress, in the Year 1861, by Harper & Brothers, in the Clerk's Office of the District Court for the Southern District of New York.

View of Fort Warren Boston harbor.

Fort Warren appeared on the cover of Harper's Weekly.
Author's Collection

to Fort Warren. These three companies were the first garrison troops at the mostly constructed, yet unfinished fort. They spent several weeks performing military drills and cleaning up the rubbish in and around the fort. They enjoyed singing popular songs of the day while working with picks, shovels and wheelbarrows.

In the evenings, they often sat around and sang songs. One of these songs was a popular Methodist camp-meeting hymn called *Say, brothers, will you meet us?* Two verses went like this:

> Say, brothers, will you meet us,
> Say, brothers, will you meet us,
> Say, brothers, will you meet us,
>   On Canaan's happy shore?
> By the grace of God we'll meet you,
> By the grace of God we'll meet you,
> By the grace of God we'll meet you,
>   Where parting is no more.

There happened to be some very good singers at the fort: Charles Edgerly, Newton J. Purnett, James Jenkins—and John Brown. Brown was of Scotch descent, a great practical joker and a good natured, well-liked soldier. The other soldiers often poked fun of him because he was the namesake of the famous abolitionist, John Brown.

The quartette and the troops often sang after the evening meal and before taps. Some of the songs of the day included: *Old Dog Tray, America, Hail Columbia,* and *Sweet Ellen Bayne* among others.

According to one version, the song began one evening when two of the members of the quartette returned to the fort. Someone shouted from the sally port, "What's the news?"

The reply was, "Why John Brown's dead."

Someone added, "But he still goes marching around."

So they began to write a song about Pvt. John Brown. A soldier named Henry Halgreen reportedly wrote the first verse:

> John Brown's body lies a-mouldering in the grave,
> His soul is marching on.
> Glory, glory, Hallelujah,
> His soul is marching on,

John Brown was a Union soldier stationed at Fort Warren.
Illustration by Jim Schmidt

Colonel Fletcher Webster, son of Daniel Webster. He was the commander of the 12th Massachusetts Regiment which made the John Brown song famous.
National Archives

He gave it to Captain James Greenleaf who was also the organist of the Harvard Church in Charlestown, Mass. Captain Greenleaf set it to the tune of *Say, brothers, will you meet us?*

At first they suggested that the name John Brown be changed to honor Colonel Ellsworth who had been recently killed at Alexandria. One of the officers was afraid that the public would think the song was glorifying the John Brown of Harper's Ferry, and they did not want to inflame the citizens. Since it was a parody song, they decided to keep the name John Brown to poke fun at their fellow, likeable soldier.

Often, when John Brown would fall into ranks late, the other soldiers would say, "Why I thought John Brown was dead!"

During the first week of May, 1861 the 12th Regiment was transferred to Fort Warren to begin training. When the Tiger Battalion was disbanded, the quartette enlisted in the 12th Massachusetts Regiment, which was known as the Webster Regiment. Brown and Jenkins went to Company A, and Purnett and Edgerly to Company E.

The 12th Massachusetts Regiment was commanded by Colonel Fletcher Webster—the son of the famous statesman, Daniel Webster. On June 26th, Colonel Webster and many of the officers and men arrived at the fort and were mustered into federal service.

One of the verses of the song came about when the men were learning to strap their overcoats to their knapsacks. John Brown was short and his knapsack was very large. The soldiers started to joke with him by saying, "Say, knapsack, where are you going with that man?" and "Guess he won't tote that load very far when we reach the Potomac."

Brown replied in his thick Scottish accent, "John Brown's knapsack is strapped upon his back, and his soul will march on as far as any of you!" This became the third verse of the song.

Soon every member of the 12th Regiment was singing the *John Brown* song at the fort. They sang the song in public for the first time as the regiment marched down State Street in Boston on the evening of July 18, 1861 and later sang it in New York and Baltimore. The Webster Regiment left the fort on July 23, 1861. Newspapers called the 12th Massachusetts, the "Psalm-singing Regiment" and the "Hallelujah Regiment." Sadly, at the Second Battle of Bull Run on August 30th, Colonel Fletcher Webster and 25 other officers and men were killed or mortally wounded.

According *The Bivouac* magazine, published in January 1885, the wartime words to the song were:

John Brown

John Brown's body lies a-mouldering in the grave,
John Brown's body lies a-mouldering in the grave,
John Brown's body lies a-mouldering in the grave,
His soul goes marching on!

Chorus   Glory, Glory, Hallelujah!
            Glory, Glory, Hallelujah!
            Glory, Glory, Hallelujah!
            His soul goes marching on!

He's gone to be a soldier in the army of the Lord,
He's gone to be a soldier in the army of the Lord,
He's gone to be a soldier in the army of the Lord,
His soul goes marching on!

John Brown's knapsack is strapped upon his back,
John Brown's knapsack is strapped upon his back,
John Brown's knapsack is strapped upon his back,
His soul goes marching on!

We'll hang Jeff Davis to a sour apple tree,
We'll hang Jeff Davis to a sour apple tree,
We'll hang Jeff Davis to a sour apple tree,
As we go marching on!

Now, three rousing cheers for the Union!
Now, three rousing cheers for the Union!
Now, three rousing cheers for the Union!
As we go marching on!

George Kimball, a soldier of Company A, of the 12th Massachusetts Regiment later wrote about the song:

> Few people aside from those who kept step to its strains when leaving home for the battlefield and sang it around the smoky camp fire during the long, dull nights and days of army life, knew the extent of its popularity and the deep hold it took upon the soldier's heart.
>
> It spread from regiment to regiment like wildfire. No song gained so firm a hold upon the troops, and it is safe to say that it was sung by every regiment—cavalry, artillery and infantry—of the Army of the Potomac.

An 1865 London newspaper published that the "great Federal war song (meaning *John Brown*) is the favorite of the people— of those who sing in the highways."

Later Julia Ward Howe composed a hymn from the same tune. The result was her famous Civil War song, *The Battle Hymn of the Republic.*

Tragically, John Brown fell off a boat and drowned while crossing the Shenandoah River near Front Royal, Virginia, in June 1862. After his death, the 12th Massachusetts Regiment never sang the *John Brown* song again. According to James Beale, a soldier of the 12th Massachusetts Regiment, when they returned to Boston in 1864, there were so few members of the original group from Fort Warren that they could not bring themselves to sing it—even for old times.

5

CONFEDERATE PRISON LIFE

One of the most notable features about Fort Warren was the humane treatment of Confederate prisoners. Because of the reports of harsh southern prisons, some citizens of Boston demanded kind treatment for the prisoners at Fort Warren. Many had hoped that if Confederate prisoners were treated kindly, the south would reciprocate and treat Union soldiers better.

Colonel Justin E. Dimick, an artillery officer, arrived in the fall of 1861 to take command of Fort Warren as previously mentioned. He had been the commander of Fort Monroe, Virginia. He was much older than most officers, and the War Department rewarded him with this easier assignment. Colonel Dimick deserves credit for the decent treatment given to Confederate prisoners. While it was far from being a four-star hotel, Fort Warren was considered

Fort Warren viewed from the town of Hull in January 2003. Nantasket Roads is in the foreground. This would have been a difficult swim, because of the strong currents, for anyone trying to escape.
Photo by Jay Schmidt

one of the better places to be imprisoned if you were a Confederate soldier, sailor or political prisoner.

Most of the prisoners at Fort Warren were there for only a relatively short time. The longest stay was under two years. If they swore allegiance, they would often be paroled. Some had trouble taking the oath of allegiance (or a variation) and other were delayed during negotiations for prisoner exchanges. Some political prisoners were released on parole to see their families. Prisoners could obtain release by a directive from either the Secretary of State or War or from his agent. Agents visited the fort and interviewed prisoners and asked about an oath of allegiance. He would forward his recommendations to federal authorities. Prisoners who refused to take the oath of allegiance, however, were usually held in high regard by other Rebel prisoners.

Lawrence Sangston, a Maryland legislator, was arrested on September 12, 1861, and eventually sent to Fort Warren. He had no love for the north, and when the ship traveled along the Massachusetts coastline, he wrote: "We never saw a more miserable and God-forsaken looking country; for hours we would not see a tree—no wonder the Yankees yearn for the South!"

He was in the first group of prisoners, and he arrived on October 31, 1861. When Sangston and the others arrived at the fort, they found Colonel Dimick apologizing for the lack of accommodations. The fort had "not a bed, nor an article of furniture of any description, and nothing to eat [for the prisoners]," wrote Sangston. Colonel Dimick sent for food in Boston and told them they would have to stay on the ship. The officers protested since they feared the men in the hold would not make it. Four hundred Confederate soldiers were then allowed into the fort despite the conditions.

Here is a letter written by a political prisoner:

FORT WARREN, BOSTON HARBOR, November 10, 1861.

Honorable W. H. SEWARD.

SIR: After some reflection I came to the conclusion to address you a few lines. I am a prisoner at this fort and have been at this and Fort Lafayette for eight weeks. I was arrested as a member of the Maryland Legislature and have understood that those arrests were made as a precautionary measure to prevent what seemed anticipated, viz, the passage of a secession ordinance. Now I pledge my honor as a man that if there were any such measure contemplated I know nothing of it nor would I have countenanced such a measure. And as I am now by virtue of the late election, a private citizen and will do nothing against the Government, I hope you will be kind enough to release me.

Yours, truly,

ANDREW KESSLER. (Signature)

The oath of allegiance the political prisoners took went like this:

I, (NAME), do solemnly swear that I will support, protect and defend the Constitution and Government of the United States against all enemies whether domestic or foreign and that I will bear true faith, loyalty and allegiance to the same, any ordinance, resolution or law of any State convention or legislature to the contrary notwithstanding; and further that I do this with a full determination, pledge and purpose and without any mental reservation or evasion whatsoever; and further that I will well and faithfully perform all the duties which may be required of me by law hereby stipulating that I will neither enter into any of the States in insurrection against the Government of the United States nor hold any correspondence whatsoever with persons residing in those States nor transmit any correspondence between any disloyal persons without permission from the Secretary of State, and also that I will not do anything hostile to the United States during the present insurrection, so help me God.

NAME (Signature)

Sworn and subscribed to before me on this the 26th day of November, 1861, at Fort Warren, Boston Harbor.

J. DIMICK, (Signature)

Colonel, U. S. Army, Commanding Post.

Colonel Justin E. Dimick, the benevolent commander of Fort Warren post and prison 1861-63.
USAMHI

Confederate prisoners and Union guards pose at the sally port.
USAMHI

Sangston's first quarters was a room sixteen by eighteen feet and was lighted by three loopholes in the granite wall about three feet long by six inches wide at the outside wall. The rooms had a small dressing room, used by all of the occupants which faced the interior of the fort. Sangston and the prisoners soon discovered that Union soldiers had taken all food, candles, soap and any useful items from their trunks and bags.

The prisoners made arrangements for delivery of Boston and New York newspapers, and Boston merchants offered them daily food catering for $1 a day. These vendors were the Civil War version of today's canteen trucks. For the first day and a half, 700 prisoners had only two hams and a box of soda crackers to share among themselves according to Sangston.

Eventually they were issued mattresses and blankets. Boston city officials later toured the fort and made note of who still needed blankets and supplied them from city funds for humanitarian reasons. Some Bostonians thought the "traitors should receive nothing."

Fort Warren was an extremely windy place because it sat on an island at the middle range of the harbor facing the open Massachusetss Bay. Sangston wrote, "At times the wind whistled through the casemate windows equal to the shrill whistle of a locomotive engine."

According to diaries some typical prisoner meals were:

Breakfast: codfish and potatoes, baked beans, pumpkin "sass" and coffee. Sunday dinner: roast turkey, mutton, roast beef, lobster salad, nuts, canned peaches, honey and coffee. The enlisted me did not eat this well. Political prisoners or military officers got this better food.

Some North Carolina officers made arrangements to get better provisions from Boston at a reasonable rate. They were even able to buy cheap Boston whiskey for $3 a gallon. Colonel Dimick permitted the prisoners to have alcohol as long as things didn't get out of hand. A favorite treat was whiskey punch in the evening. Political prisoners and Confederate officers often visited each other's quarters to share the brew. Because of his kindness, it was said that all of the prisoners without exception spoke well of Colonel Dimick.

The sally port has not basically changed in over 150 years. All prisoners had to pass through this portal. This is the view from inside the fort. The date 1850 signifies the year when the bulk of the fort was completed.
Photo by Jay Schmidt

Sangston was able to order comfort items from Boston. He bought a carpet mat, chairs, washstand, bowl and pitcher, water bucket, foot bath and a writing table with damask cloth cover. He mentioned that "... many visitors came in to view and admire ..." his tastefully furnished quarters.

The Confederate officers were held in "Officers Quarters" which consisted of rooms above and below ground. Half the rooms faced the parade ground and the rear faced an embankment (the coverface) about 30 feet high and the ditch. The lower rooms were 10 feet below the level of the parade ground. The lower rooms had stone floors, while the upper rooms had wooden plank flooring. All had closets of varying sizes.

Eventually the enlisted prisoners were issued cotton sacks, 12 pounds of straw and a blanket. They were issued standard soldier's rations and a boiler. Each casemate had a large iron kettle with a stove under it just outside the door. They would boil meat, soup and coffee in them while standing outside exposed to the weather. In his diary, Sangston mentioned seeing them thinly clad, cooking outdoors in driving rain or snow.

If Confederate officers pledged not to try to escape, they generally had free access to most of the fort. At 10 P.M. they would have to return to their quarters. The political prisoners, on the other hand, were locked up at sunset which infuriated them.

Sangston angrily wrote in his diary: "Why prisoners taken with arms in their hands in open hostility to the Government should be accorded privileges and a higher grade of treatment than those who are arrested and confined without any charge whatsoever, or ever having committed any hostile act, is one of the mysteries of 'State' or rather of 'Seward' policy I am not able to solve."

In desperation, Sangston wrote this letter:

FORT WARREN, November 16, 1861.

I have twice taken the oath to support and defend the Constitution of the United States during the present year and am not disposed to turn a solemn obligation into ridicule by constant repetitions of it.

Confederate prisoners were allowed to use the parade ground as an exercise field. Bastion B is at the center of the photo taken in 1996.
Photo by Jay Schmidt

I am not conscious of having in any way or manner violated that obligation. If I have or if the Government supposes I have, I have a right, as a citizen of the United States to demand an investigation.

I cannot by the acceptance of conditions for my release acknowledge by implication or inference that any just or legal cause existed for my arrest which I utterly deny.

I am willing to hold myself in readiness to meet any charges that may be brought against me.

LAWRENCE SANGSTON (Signature)

Sangston later met and often shared whiskey punch with Mason and Slidell, the famous participants of the Trent Affair mentioned later in this book. Sangston was paroled on January 12, 1862.

Later, Sangton's parole was extended, and he did not have to return to Fort Warren again. His diary about imprisonment at Fort Warren and other forts, *The Bastiles* [sic] *of the North* was published in 1863. An excellent copy exists at the Boston Public Library's rare book section. Copies sometimes surface at rare book dealers.

> DEPARTMENT OF STATE,
>
> Washington, January 29, 1862.
>
> Colonel JUSTIN DIMICK, Fort Warren, Boston Harbor.
>
> COLONEL: Major-General Dix has been authorized by this Department to extend the parole of Lawrence Sangston and to request him to report to him [General Dix] at Baltimore instead of to you at Fort Warren.
>
> I am, colonel, &c.,
>
> F. W. SEWARD,
>
> Assistant Secretary.

Colonel Bradford, who was captured at Hatteras Inlet and taken to Fort Warren, was one of the officers under Sylvanus Thayer, the engineer who constructed Fort Warren. It was apparently a source of amusement to the Union guards.

Between December 1861, and February 1862, most of the North Carolina prisoners were exchanged. By July 1862, most of the Fort Donelson prisoners were also paroled and sent south.

If a prisoner received parole, he could not take up arms again under the rules of war. If a prisoner had been exchanged for a Union prisoner, he was allowed to fight again.

When prisoners were at the fort, Union guards and Confederate prisoners often chatted about battles and political issues. In once instance a group of Confederates broke out into *Dixie*. Union soldiers retaliated by counter-singing and shouting which Colonel Dimick quickly stopped.

The living conditions, however, were not mentioned in high regard by the prisoners. Some initially lacked straw and bedding, others were overcrowded. In general, as some of the prisoners moved out during the various releases and exchange programs, conditions improved for the remaining prisoners with less over-crowding.

Boston newspapers urged their readers to send bedding to the prisoners in the hopes that Southerners would reciprocate and send bedding to Union prisoners. Mayor Wightman of Boston, in 1861, sent clothing, blankets, medicine, cocoa and guava jelly from the Evans House, a charitable institution established to aid Union soldiers. He got into some political hot water because of this when some of his opponents accused him of comforting the enemy.

Gifts from friends, relatives and sympathizers in the Southern or border states and charitable people in Boston arrived often at Fort Warren. The items included religious books, blankets, clothing, liquor, jelly and medicine. Around the holidays, the number of gifts to prisoners increased. Some generous Bostonians had to defend themselves against being called "pro-Confederate" because of their humanitarian gestures.

Prisoners were also allowed to attend religious services in both the casemates and open air. Local ministers often came out for services at the fort.

There was a medium-sized hospital at the fort in Bastion D, and the prisoners said it was cleaner and better smelling than the prisoners' living quarters. They joked that it was good to get sick—so that you could have better living conditions. Later in World War II, the hospital area was used for a post exchange.

Although only 13 prisoners died at Fort Warren (out of the 2,200 who were incarcerated there at one time or another), prisoners received the best medical care possible. Bostonians were concerned mostly about the supplies and conditions at the hospital. One of the prisoners, Dr. Charles Magill treated his fellow prisoners with the permission of the commander. Typhoid fever and mumps epidemics resulted in the hospitalization of many prisoners.

Both the military and political prisoners respected the benevolent Colonel Dimick. His son, Lieutenant Justin Dimick, also stationed at Fort Warren, soon received orders to report to the front. The prisoners were also fond of Lt. Dimick, and they gave him a letter requesting that Confederate soldiers give him preferential treatment in the event that he was captured. Lt. Dimick, unfortunately, was mortally wounded at Chancellorsville.

Confederate prisoners entertained themselves mostly by writing letters. They were allowed to write as often as they wished with little, if any, censorship. Incoming mail, however, was checked.

Letters with statements bordering on treason were not delivered to the prisoners. Some prisoners such as Dr. Magill wrote daily letters to his wife. They also amused themselves by visiting other prisoners, playing music, card games and making trinkets. They also used the parade ground as an exercise field.

Because of failing health, Colonel Dimick left his command at Fort Warren on November 25, 1863. He was relieved by Major Stephen Cabot of the First Batallion Massachusetts Heavy Artillery.

6

THE TRENT AFFAIR

During the Civil War, there were numerous skirmishes, battles and diplomatic conflicts. One of these famous political incidents was known as the Trent Affair—and Fort Warren played a leading role. Confederate President Jefferson Davis expected to get the Europeans to sympathize with the Southern cause and perhaps to join with them in the fight. To accomplish this, he dispatched two distinguished Southerners as commissioners: James. M. Mason was to go to England, and John Slidell was to be the Confederate commissioner to France.

Captain Charles Wilkes, commander of the USS San Jacinto, *a Union sloop of war.*
National Archives

Mason, a Virginian, and a former Senator, traveled with Slidell, a former Senator from Louisiana. They sailed on the blockade runner *Theodora* from Charleston, South Carolina, on October 12, 1861 and headed for Cuba to eventually sail to Europe. In Cuba, they soon booked passage on the British mail steamer *Trent*. The USS *San Jacinto*, a Union sloop commanded by Captain Charles Wilkes was in Havana in October. He believed that he had the right to stop and search a ship in international waters if he thought that contraband was on board. Since there was no instant communication between naval

43

Confederate Commissioner James Murray Mason.
National Archives

ships and Washington at that time, U.S. Navy captains had to make their own decisions on the spot—and Wilkes declined to check with authorities before heading out.

On November 8, 1861, the USS *San Jacinto* waiting on station in the Bahama Channel, intercepted, stopped and boarded the *Trent* with an armed detail of marines. Mason and Slidell, along with their secretaries Eustis and McFarland, were forcibly removed from the *Trent* and taken to Fort Monroe by Captain Wilkes. He graciously gave up his cabin to them. Later, Mason and Slidell and their secretaries were all transferred to Fort Warren.

Lawrence Sangston was a witness to their arrival at Fort Warren and wrote in his diary:

"Nov. 24 At eleven o'clock this morning, the steamer *San Jacinto*, [commanded by] Captain Wilkes, arrived with her prisoners, Messrs. Mason and Slidell, and Messrs. Eustis and MacFarland; their secretaries, who were duly installed in their quarters; they looked pleasant and cheerful, and a stranger might have supposed they were visitors instead of prisoners.

After delivering them, Captain Wilkes took his ship up to Boston to receive the promised ovation, and aid the loyal and patriotic people of that city in making asses of themselves."

Mason and Slidell were treated very well, and they were confined to living quarters near the sally port. The quarters, which were originally designed for an officer's family to use, had a living room with a fireplace, one or two small middle rooms, a closet and a back kitchen area.

Meanwhile, Captain Wilkes received a commendation from Congress and acclaim from Union supporters for his actions. The British, *Confederate Commissioner John Slidell*
National Archives

however, were not amused. They dispatched 11,500 troops to Canada, and the British fleet was put on notice. The English sent an ultimatum to the U.S. Government demanding the release of Mason and Slidell and the removal of Captain Wilkes from naval service. Lord Lyons requested that Mason and Slidell be placed on board an English ship, once again, under the protection of the British flag. This famous incident became known as the Trent Affair.

President Abraham Lincoln did not want to fight two wars at the same time; so the prisoners were released on January 1, 1862 under orders from Secretary of State William H. Seward. The entire Fort Warren garrison turned their backs on the departing dignitaries who boarded a small tugboat and were later transferred off Provincetown to the British sloop *Rinaldo* in a raging snowstorm. Although the Trent Affair was officially over, British troops arrived in North American waters shortly before Mason and Slidell's release. Although war had been averted between Britain and the United States, many of the troops remained in Canada.

Mason and Slidell were believed to have been imprisoned in this room. Later, Alexander Stephens, Vice President of the Confederacy, would also be incarcerated in quarters similar to this.
Photo by Jay Schmidt

Mason was later treated with indifference by the British Cabinet, and his mission never succeeded. Slidell met with Napoleon III, but he also failed to gain French support for the Confederacy.

The Trent Affair was a significant historical and political episode which helped place Fort Warren in American history books.

7

FAMOUS CONFEDERATE PRISONERS

Fort Warren's place in American history was achieved primarily because of the many high-level and important Confederate military and political prisoners who were incarcerated within its walls during the war between the states. Prisoners began arriving at the fort in October, 1861. Dozens of prominent Southerners, both civilian and military, were sent to Fort Warren throughout the war. The political prisoners at that time were often held by the federal government without charges or trials.

According to some sources, prisoners from the following states were incarcerated at Fort Warren:

Alabama
Arkansas
Florida
Georgia
Kentucky
Louisiana
Maryland (political)
Mississippi
Missouri
North Carolina
Pennsylvania (political)
South Carolina
Tennessee
Texas
Virginia
West Virginia

General Simon Bolivar Buckner, CSA.
National Archives

General Simon Bolivar Buckner (1823–1914)

General Buckner was a former West Point philosophy professor and arrived at Fort Warren in March 1862 after he surrendered Fort Donelson, Tenn., to "Unconditional Surrender" Grant. Buckner, a former associate of Colonel Dimick, arrived at the fort, and the next day Dimick received orders for Buckner to be placed in solitary confinement. Colonel Dimick reportedly was reduced to tears and had to be consoled by Buckner himself.

When Generals Buckner and Tilghman arrived in Boston, the papers at that time wrote that they were jeered by the citizens of the city. He was exchanged in August 1862. After the war, Buckner, with no ill feelings, later served as one of President Grant's pallbearers.

General Richard S. Ewell, CSA
Library of Congress

General Richard S. Ewell (1817–1872)

Richard Stoddert Ewell was graduated from West Point in 1840 and served in the Mexican War. In the Civil War, he resigned to join the Confederacy, and he commanded a Confederate division under Stonewall Jackson in the 2nd Corps of the Army of Northern Virginia. In August 1862, he lost his leg at Groveton, Va. He returned to command the 2nd Corps after the death of Jackson in May 1863. At the Battle of Gettysburg, he attacked the Union forces on Culp's Hill and Cemetery Ridge on the evening of July 2, 1863. He was relieved of field command in May 1864 due to injury and was appointed to command the defense of Richmond. After the evacuation of the Confederate capital, he fought again with the Army of Northern Virginia until his capture at the Battle of Sayler's Creek in April 1865. He was held as a prisoner of war at Fort Warren until mid July 1865.

Brig. General Eppa Hunton (1823–1908)

Eppa Hunton, a Virginian, was a former schoolteacher and lawyer who joined the Confederate cause. A colonel at Gettysburg, he was wounded (halfway during the charge) and his horse killed while leading his command in Pickett's famous charge against the Union forces, where his men were nearly all killed, wounded or captured. At Sayler's Creek on April 6, 1865, Brigadier General Hunton was captured by Federal infantry with most of his men when Custer's Union cavalry halted their retreat. He was sent to Fort Warren along with General Ewell where they both remained prisoners until that July.

General Hunton wrote in his journal:

> Our mess at Fort Warren consisted of seven general officers: General Ewell, General Kershaw, General Corse, General Barton, General Wilson, General DuBose and myself. Six other prisoners (among them General Cabell of Arkansas, but a native of Virginia) were there and had access to our room.

> One day I was asleep in bed in my room when I was aroused by a commotion and found that the 12 Confederate officers were having a meeting. I inquired what it meant and was told that, to my great indignation, that it was a meeting called by General Ewell to declare, by resolution, that they had no complicity in the death of Abraham Lincoln and deplored the act. I asked them if they thought that 13 gentlemen who were thought worthy to wear the stars of general officers of the Confederate Army to declare to the world that they were not assassins. By great exertions, and by the aid of several that came to my aid, the resolution was defeated.

> I asked General Ewell where the leg he lost at Manassas was buried for I wished to honor it, for I had none to pay to the rest of his body. He replied that he didn't know where it was.

George Proctor Kane (1820–1878)

George P. Kane was the police marshall of Baltimore, Maryland, who tried to protect Union troops from mob attacks. He was arrested by Federal soldiers and later imprisoned at Fort Warren for thirteen months. After his release, he returned to Maryland where he was sheriff of Baltimore in 1873, and mayor at the time of his death in 1878.

Alexander Hamilton Stephens, Vice President of the Confederacy (1812–1883)

Alexander Stephens, also known as "Little Aleck," was born in 1812 in Georgia. He was constantly in poor health and suffered from a number of medical problems. He was a lawyer, and at the outbreak of the Civil War (although anti-secession) he was elected as Vice President of the Confederacy. Following the defeat of the south, he was arrested on May 11, 1865 at his home in Crawfordville, Georgia.

Stephens was sent to Fort Warren along with John H. Reagan, Postmaster General of the Confederate States of America. They reached Boston Harbor at eleven o'clock on the night of May 24, 1865. Stephens wrote an extensive and detailed diary during his confinement at Fort Warren titled *Recollections of Alexander H. Stephens* which was reprinted in 1998 and is still available in paperback as of this writing.

Here are some excerpts from his diary which describe prisoner life at the fort.

> May 25.—Lieutenant Woodman brought me immediately inside the fort. After going through the sally port and descending some stone steps, he stopped at the first room to the left saying, "This is your room," or "These are your quarters." I forget which. I surveyed the room. A coal fire was burning; a table and chair were in the centre; a narrow, iron, bunk-like bedstead with mattress and covering was in a corner. The floor was stone—large square blocks. The door was locked. For the first time in my life I had the full realization of being a prisoner. I was alone.
>
> May 27.—Took short walk out this morning with Lieut. Woodman. Rain drove me in. Greatly depressed about home and the dear ones there, though I have not

John H. Reagan, Postmaster General, Confederate States of America.
Library of Congress

suffered such agony as yesterday. Gave an order on Lieut. Ray in payment for certain articles which have been brought me. These, with prices are as follows:

1 lb. coffee, 80 cts; teaspoon, 37 cts; condensed milk, 75 cts; 1 lb. B, sugar, 25 cts; 1 lb., W, sugar, 30 cts; 1 lb. B. tea, $2; matches 4 cts; scissors, $1; pitcher 75 cts; mirror, 50 cts; candlestick, 37 cts; blankbook, $2; vial ink, 15 cts; steel pens, 15 cts; lead pencil, 20 cts; spittoon,

75 cts; 1 pk. Irish potatoes, 50 cts; cup and saucer, 50 cts; box for potatoes, 25 cts; coffee-pot, $2; washstand, $2; 1 lb. candles, 60 cts; in all $16.23. The sutler's name is A. J. Hall.

Stephens was still confined to the lower casemates near the sally port at this time.

June 2.—As I was walking in my room just now a number of persons,—men, women and children—appeared on the stone walk directly in front of my windows. The walk is on a solid wall about eight feet from the wall of my cell, allowing a passage for the guards. The guards' beat is on the same level with my floor, but the level of the walk is that of the drill-ground and on the same plane with the top of my windows. By peeping down, these persons could see me as in each round I approached and passed my windows ... This is the first time I have been gazed at by any persons with only a view to gratify curiosity, since my arrest.

June 14.—Walked out at 6:15. Saw Jackson and DuBose on the opposite bastion—too far to recognize them. Lieut. W[oodman] told me who they were. Saw General Ewell on his crutches. He was walking on [the] parapet. I remarked that I thought Ewell had an artificial leg; wondered [why] he did not use it. Lieut. W[oodman] replied that Ewell said he was waiting before getting an artificial leg to see if the authorities were going to hang him; if he was going to be hung, he did not care to go to the expense; intended to wait and make out on his crutches until that matter was decided. Ewell has a sense of humour.

Stephens, although in ill health, exercised by walking around in his room and wrote a description of a typical Fort Warren meal at that time.

June 23.—I have walked a mile and upward in my room; that is, 1,900 steps, which with my stride, I have no doubt would make a mile in a direct line . . . The room or cell, 24 x 20 feet, offers space for a good walk by moving in a circle.

Alexander H. Stephens, Vice President of the Confederate States (1861-65).
National Archives

Dinner: salmon, lamb, peas, snap-beans, turnips, pota-toes, bread, ice-cream and other confections about which I can give no other information than that they were palat-able, though I barely tasted of them. The ice-cream was my first this season; being a little apprehensive of bad effects, I finished with a pretty stiff drink from Harry's bottle—about two tablespoonfuls.

He also described the duties of the Union soldiers who guard him and his empathy for them.

> June 26.—Sitting at my window, smoking my meerschaum, my mind went into reverie on my present situation; especially the absurdity and foolery of it. This was suggested by the passing of the guard to and fro, with his loaded musket and glistening bayonet, peeping in occasionally, to see if I am safe, I suppose. The unceasing step of the guard is as regular as the tick of a clock. It is kept up day and night. One man is on the beat for two hours: then he is relieved by another who paces two hours; and so on: being relieved for four hours, when he must return and act as before for another two hours. One set detailed for guard duty goes through these rounds for twenty-four hours, then another set is detailed for twenty-four, the same set performing guard duty about two days in the week. The conduct of these men is often the subject of my attention; they not infrequently have my sympathy and commiseration. They are not allowed to sit or rest, but must walk to and fro, about fifteen paces, all the time.

He then described the procedure when guards are relieved.

> The relief is well known some distance off by footsteps on the stone pavement . . . The guard on duty wheels about, faces the front with the musket duly presented, crying out, "Who comes here?" The officer in charge of the relief replies, "Relief!" Whereupon the guard on duty says, "Advance, relief!" Up comes the officer with the new guard, asks the one about to be relieved sundry questions, such as, "What is the news?" or "Is there anything new?"

On July 29, he was finally released from solitary confinement.

> I am allowed to go in and out at pleasure, and walk the grounds when I choose, between sunrise and sunset; see any members of my family or any of my personal friends and converse with officers and persons in the fort besides those having special charge of me. In other words I am simply put on parole in the fort. Lieut. Newton soon

came . . . and immediately took the lock off my door.
No language can express the relief that sound gave me—
the sound of the clanking iron as it fell upon my ears.

General Grant visited Faneuil Hall in Boston in July 1865.
Stephens had great admiration for the Union general.

> July 31.—Sunday's *Herald* and this morning's *Post*
> describe his arrival in Boston on Saturday. General Grant
> is a remarkable man and, if he lives and continues in good
> health, will figure largely in the future of the country.
> I consider him one of the most remarkable men I ever
> saw.

Stephens was still confined to the lower casemates until
President Johnson ordered that he be moved to more comfortable quarters. He was then transferred to better accommodations
above ground at the parade ground level in the same type of
quarters where Mason and Slidell had been confined several years
earlier.

> Aug. 20.—I am in my new quarters. I am out of the hole.
> I am on deck. I am in a comfortable room with fair and
> beautiful prospect out toward the South and rejoicing
> in a brilliant sunlight . . . The apartments consist of
> three rooms, a sort of parlour, in which I now am,
> fronting south, a room in the rear in which my bed is
> placed, a neat and comfortable bedroom. By opening
> doors and windows, we have a draft all through the
> rooms. The new arrangement suits me admirably. I
> doubt if I could, as to rooms, be more comfortable in any
> hotel in Boston or New York. The removal is from a cell
> to a palace as far as comfort is concerned.

On October 12, 1865, his orders for release finally came
through.

> October 13. —I rose early and now make this last entry.
> I expect to start by this evening's boat for my dear home.
> It is a long and hazardous trip for me, beset with many
> dangers. But, O God in whom I put my trust, deliver me
> from all evil.

Stephens was released on parole from Fort Warren on October 13, 1865. He was the most famous Confederate prisoner ever held at Fort Warren. In 1882 he was elected governor of Georgia, but he died during his term on March 4, 1883.

General Lloyd Tilghman (1816–1863)

General Lloyd Tilghman was graduated from West Point in the class of 1836 and later became a civil engineer for several railroad companies. He joined Confederate service in the Civil War and briefly commanded both Fort Henry and Fort Donelson. As commander of Fort Henry, Tenn., he stayed with his troops until they were forced to surrender to General Ulysses S. Grant in early February 1862. He was sent to Fort Warren along with many of his officers. Tilghman was later released by prisoner exchange and commanded the First Brigade of Loring's Division in the Confederate Army of the West. He was killed in action at the Battle of Champion's Hill during the defense of Vicksburg on May 16, 1863.

General Isaac R. Trimble (1802–1888)

Isaac R. Trimble was graduated from West Point in 1822. He resigned his commission and worked in the railroad business. As an officer he achieved many victories for the Confederacy. After the battle of Gettysburg in July 1863, where he lost a leg, Trimble was brought to Fort Warren. He remained at Fort Warren until early in February 1865 when he was exchanged. After his exchange, he tried to join Lee's forces, but reached Lynchburg on April 10—the day after Appomattox.

Some other prominent Confederate prisoners at Fort Warren included General Adam R. Johnson and General Thomas Benton Smith. Harry Gilmore, who became a writer and, later, police commissioner of Baltimore was also a prisoner. Commodore John Randolph Tucker, the entire board of Baltimore Police Commissioners and many Maryland legislators served time at the fort.

General Isaac R. Trimble, CSA.
National Archives

During the early Civil War years, some Confederate prisoners passed around autograph books for fellow prisoners to sign. The signatures included Mason and Slidell.

General Thomas Benton Smith, CSA
National Archives

Several original copies of the autograph book have been preserved. One is located at the Army Military History Institute at Carlisle, Pennsylvania, one is at the Maryland Historical Society and one is kept by the Metropolitan District Commission (MDC) in Boston.

8

CONFEDERATE ESCAPES

The most famous escape from Fort Warren involved sailors from the CSS *Atlanta* and the CSS *Tacony*. The CSS *Atlanta* was a vessel built in Scotland and converted to a Confederate ironclad ram having previously been used as a blockade runner. It was purchased by the Confederates after making it through the Union blockade. It left the Savannah River and headed just outside the harbor at Savannah, Ga., under the command of Captain William A. Webb. On the morning of June 17, 1863, they ran aground on a sand bar while attempting to outrun the Union monitor *Weehawken* and surrendered after a brief pounding.

The crew was captured, and they ended up at Fort Warren. 1st Lt. Joseph W. Alexander wrote, "The officers and men always

The Confederate ironclad CSS Atlanta. *After being captured by the U.S. Navy it was later renamed the USS* Atlanta.
U.S. Naval Historical Center

treated us kindly. At first we were allowed to purchase anything we wished. And for a while our friends in Baltimore and some in Boston sent us many things, clothing and eatables, but after a time, acting under orders from Washington, we were not allowed to buy anything and had only the rations usually allowed prisoners, which were neither plentiful nor inviting."

There were also officers and men from the CSS *Tacony* imprisoned at the same time. The prisoners were confined in the casemates and were allowed to exercise out on the parade ground during the day, but restricted to quarters with a guard outside at night.

Four of them decided to try to escape from the solid granite fort. Beside Lt. Alexander, the others included 2nd Lt. Charles. W. Reed (sometimes spelled Read) of the CSS *Tacony*, Lieutenant of Marines James Thurston also of the CSS *Atlanta* and Reid Sanders (sometimes spelled Saunders), a political prisoner from Kentucky.

The men noticed the huge musketry loopholes (about six feet high and three feet wide on the interior narrowing down to a much smaller opening about seven inches wide on the exterior scarp wall). Alexander found that by turning his head he could squeeze through the opening. Remember, these men were smaller than the average men today. The lower end was about ten feet from the ditch bottom. The fort was built for defense, not for holding prisoners, so the fort's designers never envisioned that anyone would try to fit through the musketry loopholes and get out of the fort.

The First Attempt

On Sunday, August, 16, 1863, the four of them slipped through one of the musketry loopholes in the room where they got their drinking water. They dropped down into a ditch near the sally port. (This room was about 70 feet away from the sally port.) Just after 9 P.M. they climbed the coverface, crept toward the seawall and found sentries walking back and forth. The escapees got to the water and were lying down with their heads against the seawall and their feet in the water. The water was very rough, and they did not think they could make it to a nearby island by swimming. The four of them decided to try again during more favorable conditions. They had left a rope hanging from the loophole in case they failed. (The prisoners had taken the canvas and ropes off their sea chests which were brought to the fort after their capture.) When they returned, another prisoner doubted that they got outside until he tasted the salt on their clothing.

Lt. Reed suggested that two of his men, Sherman and Pryde, who were excellent swimmers, be allowed to go with them. They would swim to a nearby island, steal a boat, and return to get their fellow prisoners.

The Escape

One night later on August 17, the original four prisoners, Reed, Sanders, Thurston and Alexander again lowered themselves and went to the seawall along with the two swimmers. Sherman and Pryde jumped into the water and swam off. Alexander said, "I heard that they made their way back to the Confederacy, but I

The Confederates made their daring escape from this area of the fort. They lowered themselves from the flank of Bastion C (left), crossed this ditch and climbed over the coverface on the right.
Photo by Jennifer Schmidt

am not certain that this is true." According to the news reports of the time, nothing had been heard from them, and it is believed that they drowned in the rough, stormy waters that night.

After waiting fruitlessly, Alexander and Thurston decided to swim over to a nearby island (Lovell's Island) west of the Narrows lighthouse known as Bug Light. This island is about a half-mile away across the Narrows shipping channel from George's Island. When they moved along the shore, they found a large pine board target, used for artillery practice, which had been pulled up on the shore. The two of them decided to put their clothes on the target and shove it ahead of them. Thurston and Alexander dragged the target to the water, but soon two Union sentries came along.

"Where is the target?" one of them said. "Wasn't it here when we came on post?" They went over to the edge where the darkest night shadows fell concealing the escapees. Alexander wrote that one of them said, "I believe I see something down here in the water. Stick your bayonet into it, and see what it is." The point of the bayonet came slowly down and actually rested on Reed's chest lying in the water. He never moved a muscle. Alexander wrote, "That was the bravest thing I saw during the four years of the war."

The soldiers concluded that "spirits had taken it away" and moved along on patrol. The Confederates decided that only two of them, Thurston and Alexander, should try to escape the island. Reed and Sanders would wait nearby until Thurston and Alexander returned for them.

The two escapees shoved off and headed for Lovell's Island keeping the lighthouse on their right as they swam across the channel in the rough, cold water. After what seemed to them to be hours in the stormy sea, they reached the island. Both of them stayed together and walked along the dark shore. Soon they found a small boat pulled up onto the beach. Thurston and Alexander pulled up the anchors and shoved the boat out. The men hoisted the sail and headed for the fort to pick up Reed and Sanders. As daylight was approaching, they planned to lower the sail and move close. Reed and Sanders were not in the designated hiding place, and Thurston and Alexander did not realize that their fellow escapees had been discovered and captured. By now, both were in close confinement.

Confederate prisoners at Fort Warren. Several sources have identified the following prisoners who were involved in the dramatic escape. Circled from left to right: Reid Sanders, a political prisoner; 2nd Lt. Charles W. Reed of the CSS Tacony; 1st Lt. Joseph W. Alexander of the CSS Atlanta; Captain William A. Webb of the CSS Atlanta (who was not involved in the actual escape). USAMHI

At daybreak, on the morning of August 18, Colonel Dimick was told that there was an escape and two had been recaptured. He ordered a roll call at once, and they soon discovered that four prisoners were missing. Colonel Dimick asked a steamer heading to Boston to notify the Boston Chief of Police and the Army's Federal Provost Marshall. He also asked them to send telegraph messages in all directions about the escape.

Colonel Dimick ordered every inch of George's Island searched for the missing prisoners. They soon learned that a sailboat belonging to a man at Lovell's Island was missing. They also found the missing target as well as some planks lashed to the target.

Meanwhile Thurston and Alexander sailed past the Federal sentinels and hoped to get to New Brunswick, Canada. The men sailed all day with little clothing, no food or water. About dark, they approached the shore at Rye Beach, N.H., and found a man with a horse. They told him that they sailed from Portsmouth, went swimming, and their clothing was blown overboard. The escapees asked him for something to eat, and he went and got them some old clothes, food, tobacco and a small bottle of cherry brandy. They did not think he believed their story, and as soon as he was out of sight, Thurston and Alexander again headed north along the coast towards Eastport, Maine.

The Capture

Meanwhile the Revenue Cutter *Dobbin* in Portland, Maine, under the command of Captain John Adams Webster, was ordered to search for the missing prisoners. After two days of attempting to sail north, Thurston and Alexander noticed a nearby schooner changing course frequently. The men soon figured out that the schooner was looking for them. The *Dobbin* pulled alongside at about noon on August 20th and started asking questions. Thurston and Alexander told the same tale about having clothing blown overboard. When the Rebels were searched, the officers found some Confederate money on Thurston, so they placed the escapees aboard the cutter (the predecessor of a modern U.S. Coast Guard cutter).

Captain Webster treated them kindly and turned them over to a U.S. Marshall when they arrived in Portland, Maine. They were quickly handcuffed and taken to the Portland city jail. Alexander said "The food furnished us in the jail was certainly the most disgusting ever offered to men."

Their friends at Fort Warren reportedly sent them some clothing. The prisoners soon became a public spectacle and caused great excitement in Portland. Everyone wanted to see the "Rebel Prisoners." After a while, Thurston and Alexander ignored the people staring and commenting about them. Both remained imprisoned in Portland for about a month on the second floor of the jail.

The two Confederates were soon figuring out how to saw through some of the bars and escape, when they were transferred back to Fort Warren. There they learned that Reed and Sanders had been caught and confined under close guard on the opposite side of the fort the same night they made their escape.

For several months, Alexander and Thurston were kept in close confinement also. The commanding officer of Fort Warren, Colonel Dimick, offered to put them with the other prisoners if they gave their word not to attempt to escape. They refused. Soon both of them were planning another escape.

After finally being returned to their old casemate, Thurston and Alexander noticed that there were two brick chimneys in the room and each had two flues. One was for the fireplace in their room, and one was for the fireplace in the adjacent room. If they removed the flues, they thought they could squeeze through and make it to the top. The men started removing bricks from inside the chimney, smashed them to bits and dumped the dust into their slop buckets for disposal. Morrell, an engineer from the *Atlanta*, would replace some bricks each morning and used bread made into dough to whitewash the bricks and to disguise the missing mortar. After several months, they discovered that Union sentinels were placed near the chimney tops which protruded a few feet into the ramparts. Alexander later wrote, "It was a bitter disappointment to us; but we did not have to bear it for a very long time, for, in September, I think it was, we were ordered to go to City Point for exchange."

Seventeen months after being captured, Lt. Alexander was exchanged on a Confederate vessel on the James River nine miles below Richmond, Virginia.

Colonel Dimick had iron bars placed on the infamous musketry loopholes to prevent further escapes. That was the last of the major prison escapes from Fort Warren.

The Demilune Escape

Another minor escape took place reportedly in October 1863. Located just outside the entrance to the sally port on the shore-side of the earthen coverface sits a large granite, semi-circular defensive fortification called a demilune or occasionally a caponniere. During the Civil War, the outside of Fort Warren's demilune was protected by a ditch about 10 feet deep.

The narrow musketry loophole on the right from which Sawyer escaped. It is partially blocked with concrete. During the Civil War there was an 8-10 foot ditch in front of this opening. It is filled in today.
Photo by Jay Schmidt

A private named Sawyer, who deserted from a Maine regiment, was confined in one of the casemates of the demilune on the right as it faced the sea. Edward Rowe Snow believed that for three weeks, Sawyer chiseled the edges of the granite musketry loophole until he was able to squeeze through and escape. (He must have been a very tiny young man.) He managed to swim out to a nearby schooner, but was later discovered and returned to the fort. His final fate is unknown.

Before World War I the demilune ditch was filled in and a road cut through the earth coverface to allow military vehicles to enter the fort easier. You can still see the musketry loophole in the demilune today. It has a patch of concrete where Private Sawyer made his escape. It is now at ground level.

A Foiled Escape Plan

In March 1864, some Confederate prisoners intended to jump a small group of Union soldiers left guarding them while the others were eating. They planned to grab some of the muskets stacked nearby and then take over the steamer tied up at the pier and make their escape. According to the Boston *Herald*, "Arrangements were also made to cut the telegraph wire leading to the city to prevent an alarm being given. Since the discovery of the plot, additional precautions have been taken to keep the prisoners more secure."

The plan was foiled when a prisoner, who had taken the oath of allegiance, told the prison authorities about the conspiracy.

9

THE EXECUTION OF DESERTERS

The maximum penalty during the Civil War for the most serious military crimes, including desertion, was death—usually by a military firing squad. There is one documented instance of a dual execution of Union deserters which took place at Fort Warren.

According to accounts in the Boston *Herald* of that time, the executions were conducted on the afternoon of April 22, 1864. Two Vermont soldiers, Matthew Riley, 23, (alias John Roach) and Charles Carpenter, 21, whose real name was believed to be James McCarty, faced a firing squad at Fort Warren.

Both men were known as "bounty jumpers." These criminals would enlist in a unit and collect a cash bounty. They would then quickly desert and enlist in another unit, often under an assumed name and collect another bounty. As soon as they were unguarded, they would desert again. Bounty jumpers were among the most hated criminals of the time. Riley and Carpenter were reportedly members of an organized gang of professional bounty swindlers.

Riley and Carpenter enlisted in the 5th Vermont Volunteers, Company E at Sunderland, Vt., in December 1863. They were transported to Brattleboro, Vt., where they each received their $200 bounty on December 5. The very next day they deserted and enlisted again in Springfield, Mass. They were headed to West Lebanon, N.H., to enlist once again, when they were finally apprehended. They each escaped and were re-captured before facing military court martial.

The General Court Martial for the two men was held at Gallop's Island in Boston Harbor. The men were found guilty and sentenced to be shot to death on Friday, April 22, 1864 at Fort Warren—where the men were being held in Bastion C.

Both men were Catholics and were given the opportunity to have a priest with them. Rev. Patrick V. Moice of St. James Church on Albany Street in Boston, came to the fort, stayed with them and prepared them to meet their fate.

Major Stephen Cabot, commanding officer of Fort Warren, was assigned to oversee the execution of the two men. He did his duty with such feeling and kindness that the prisoners expressed their thanks to him. On the morning of the executions, Riley's mother, father and cousin took an early boat to the fort to be with him as did Carpenter's mother, fiancé and a friend who also came to the fort that morning. They met briefly with the condemned men and were sent back on the return trip.

Both men had petitioned for a reprieve and Major Cabot even held off the execution in case one came through. None did.

At one o'clock in the afternoon, it was time for the execution to begin. All five companies at the fort, in full dress uniform, formed on the fort's parade ground. They marched through the sally port, past the guardhouse and around to a flat area on the north side of the fort near the demilune. The companies formed three sides of a square. Major Cabot commanded the battalion accompanied by Dr. Severance, the Surgeon of the Post. Among the members of the battalion were 37 prisoners, under guard, to observe the execution in the hopes that it would have an effect on them. Witnesses said that some of these men were more nervous than Carpenter and Riley.

While the battalion was forming up, a squad, along with the band of the First U.S. Artillery which played the Dead March, went to where the prisoners were held. This procession also included the firing squad. Their two coffins were carried on a bier and the prisoners followed, manacled together with a two foot chain, and accompanied by Father Moice. The procession also included 16 privates with two non-commission officers, with arms reversed.

The men marched along by their own fresh dug graves and gave no indication of any reaction. Once the procession was in place, the coffins were set on the ground and the men were placed between them. The firing squad moved into place, six paces in front of the men. Father Moice attended to the kneeling prisoners.

The Execution Order

Lieutenant Ray then read the following execution order from their court martial:

> The Major General Commanding approves the proceedings, findings, and sentences in the case of Private Charles Carpenter and Matthew Riley, alias John Roach, unassigned recruits for volunteers.
>
> The crime of which these men are convicted is among the most heinous in the military code. They were confederated with three other persons to enlist, obtain the bounty and desert the service of the Government immediately after swearing allegiance to it. The recruiting officers were warned of their intention, but not withstanding every precaution, they succeeded, the day after they were mustered into service, in effecting their escape. Carpenter, after his desertion, dyed his hair and disguised himself, and commenced the business of

The companies formed on this parade ground and marched out to the execution site to await the prisoners.
Photo by Jay Schmidt

Bounty and Substitute Broker, Riley was one of his confederates in enlisting and deserting, and they were found
together when they were arrested, the continued asso-
ciation indicated that they were league together for the
commission of further crimes.

Desertion is, in all services, one of the most flagrant
of military crimes. It is compounded of perjury, infidelity to the Government and a cowardly abandonment
of the National flag. In season of public peril it puts
on its darkest aspect. It is, so far as the guilty perpe-
trator can make it, the surrender of the cause of the
country to its enemies. In these cases it was compli-
cated with the base and premeditated purpose of
defrauding the Treasury by a pretended engagement in
the military service of the country, to be followed by
an immediate repudiation of it.

At a period when the Government is making the
strongest appeals to the people to rally to its support
against the desperate efforts of its enemies to destroy it,
a class of men, regardless of all moral obligations, and
of all the instincts of honor and patriotism, are thrusting
themselves into the service for the purpose of making
a mercenary profit out of the public necessities, and set-
ting and example of falsehood and infidelity calculated
to dissolve all the ties which should bind a community
together in the hour of adversity and peril.

It is due to the course of public justice that this example should be rebuked, and that the prevalence of desertion should be checked, if the infliction of the highest
penalty of the law can restrain it; and the Major General
commanding hereby announces his determination to
carry into execution with unyielding firmness the sentence of death when it shall be deliberately pronounced
in such cause, after a fair and impartial trial, and when
in his judgment, the crime shall have been clearly proved.
However painful the duty, every consideration of public
justice and public policy demands that it should be
inflexibly performed.

Privates Carpenter and Riley, alias Roach, will be shot to death at Fort Warren, in the harbor of Boston, Mass., on Friday, the 22nd day of April instant, between the hours of noon and 2 o'clock P.M. The commanding officer of Fort Warren is charged with the execution of this order.

By command of Major Gen. Dix

D.T. Van Buren.

Col. and Assistant Adjutant General

The firing squad consisted of 20 men, four from each of the five companies. Some of them were taken out and moved to the rear in reserve. The actual execution detail was comprised of two squads of eight men—each group commanded by a sergeant. One of the rifles in each squad was loaded with a blank as was the military custom at that time.

The prisoners were marched down this road from the sally port. (The WW II configuration of the sally port bridge is in the center of the photo.) The fort's earthen coverface can be seen clearly on the left. They marched around to the other side of this coverface, near the demilune, and were shot by a firing squad.
Photo by Jay Schmidt

The Execution

Lieutenant Ray then asked the men if they wanted to say anything, but they declined. Father Moice again prayed with them and moved away.

The *Herald* reported the actual execution:

> The Provost Marshall and the two sergeants of the firing party then went to them and took off the manacles; the prisoners were ordered to take off their coats and vests, which they promptly did, and then their hands were pinioned behind and their eyes bandaged with white cloths.
>
> Each was then requested to rest on one knee and this was also promptly done, neither party exhibiting the slightest nervousness. The Provost Marshall and his assistants immediately left them, and without a moment's delay the orders *"Ready," "Aim," "Fire"* were given by Lieut. Batchelder, and the two men fell at full length backwards dead, the body of Riley being pierced with seven bullets, all in the region of the heart, and that of Carpenter with six, all but one in the same locality.

After the execution, Dr. Severance, the Surgeon, pronounced them both dead after he conducted a brief examination. The firing squad withdrew, and the entire battalion marched past the bodies back into the fort. A work detail unbound the hands, removed the blindfolds and placed the bodies in the coffins. Major Cabot approved the request from relatives to have the bodies returned to them. Soldiers placed the two coffins into pine boxes inside a storehouse, and they were later transported by the evening boat to Boston. The bodies were shipped, at Government expense, to relatives.

The Execution Site

As in the Civil War, the fort has an earthen bank (coverface) masking its north and east scarp walls which forms the outer side of the ditch protecting the north side of the demilune. This huge earth coverface served as an ideal backdrop during the execution to trap any stray bullets.

The execution site of Riley and Carpenter, which is the flat area to the side of the demilune, is now a picnic area. This writer believes the two deserters were executed in front of the coverface on the right of the demilune as you face it—with the fort in the background.

The companies formed three sides of a square in this area for the execution. The prisoners were believed to have been shot in front of this part of the coverface.
Photo by Jennifer Schmidt

10

FROM THE CIVIL WAR
THROUGH WORLD WAR I

After the Civil War, Fort Warren had only about 300 soldiers on duty, and it still remained an active, but small post. The army also realized that the rifled, modern artillery, at that time, would easily pound the granite structure to pieces. They would, by the mid 1890s, slowly start replacing some of the outmoded cannons with concrete batteries which were the state-of-the-art fortifications at the turn of the century.

An early 20th century postcard showing several wooden buildings which no longer exist.
Author's Collection

A 12-inch disappearing rifle gun tube for Battery Stevenson in front of the brick guardhouse just after the turn of the century. In the foreground are two 10-inch Rodman cannons sleeved down to 8-inch rifle tubes. The Civil War guardhouse is on the left.
USS Salem Archives

Transporting one of the 12-inch gun tubes for Battery Stevenson in the early 1900s. The photo has been mistakenly labeled as a 10-inch gun. The mine storage building is in the background.
National Archives

Following the Civil War the fort, however, was still heavily armed. In 1885 records from the fort indicate the following guns were present:

Located in the casemates:
- Two 8-inch converted rifles
- Twenty-three 24-pounder howitzers

Mounted *en barbette*:
- Five 15-inch Rodman smoothbores
- Ninety-six 10-inch Rodman smoothbores
- Two 8-inch converted rifles
- One 200-pounder Parrott rifle
- One 100-pounder Parrott rifle

The Endicott Period

The huge 15-inch Rodman smoothbore cannons developed in the 1850s were obsolete by the 1870s. Powerful 9- to 14-inch rifled

Battery Bartlett which once held four 10-inch disappearing rifles. It is currently off-limits to visitors because of its deteriorating condition. The #4 gun emplacement was removed to repair the seawall in 1976. Photo by Jay Schmidt

guns were being mounted on some European iron warships. In the 1880s, the Endicott Board (chaired by Secretary of War, William C. Endicott) recommended new fortifications and the construction of new forts to defend many coastal U.S. cities. Fort Warren was selected to receive several new gun battery upgrades. The often massive concrete emplacements designed at that time generally held one to four guns of a standard caliber and size protected by earthen parapets. These batteries were not visible from the sea because of their low profile, and they protected the gun crews by the emplacement design. Mechanical hoists were used to move powder and shells up to the platforms as needed.

By the early 1890s, the army haltingly started to give Fort Warren a major facelift. From an obsolete granite-walled fort, with dozens of muzzle-loading cannon, Fort Warren turned into a modern (for that time) coast defense fortification with massive concrete batteries with high-powered and accurate breech-loading coast rifles.

Battery Lowell was armed with three 3-inch rapid fire guns on balanced-pillar mounts during the Spanish-American War through World War I. It is located outside of the granite walls of the fort.
Photo by Jay Schmidt

Battery Stevenson had two 12-inch disappearing rifles. This is gun emplacement #1. These were the most powerful guns ever installed at Fort Warren. This battery was in use until late in World War II.
Photo by Jay Schmidt

These new "Endicott Period" batteries did not have to be placed inside the protective walls of a masonry fort anymore. They could be located almost anywhere along the shore for effective coverage since they, themselves, were heavily fortified. During this period, Battery Bartlett and Battery Lowell were built outside of Fort Warren's granite walls. Battery Jack Adams, Battery Plunkett and Battery Stevenson were constructed atop the fort by modifying the granite structure itself with tons of concrete.

In 1895, a reporter from *The Bostonian* visited the fort and wrote:

> On the northern and eastern sides of Fort Warren, fortifications of solid concrete are being constructed that shall, when finished, and manned with their twelve inch guns [actually 10-inch], make a defense that will practically intercept the entrance of foreign warships past their frowning fortresses to the harbor beyond. These concrete parapets are to be finished with a covering of earth, which, when green sodded, will form an exterior so innocent and beautiful in its terraced appearance ... that can ... vomit forth terrible destruction.

This single mount, Battery Jack Adams, was constructed of such poor concrete that the 10-inch disappearing rifle was used only briefly. It was disarmed about 1914. It is located in Bastion B, and it was one of the first Endicott Period batteries erected in the country.
Photo by Jay Schmidt

The writer is referring to the 10-inch disappearing gun batteries of Jack Adams and Bartlett #1 and #2 which were soon installed as concrete modifications to the fort's Bastion B's ramparts and the southern half of the ravelin, respectively.

The writer continued:

> Facing the parade [ground], on the north side, are the quarters of the privates with rooms extending from the casemates to the buttress, furnished with 10 beds, with good springs and mattresses, and covered with gray army blankets. On a shelf over each bed are neatly folded the various uniforms of the soldiers, while between are hung the knapsacks for clothing, canteen for water or coffee, haversack for rations, and the cartridge-belt. A barracks-box for extra clothing is also allowed each man. The rooms are heated by stoves, and a sink at the farther end and the stack of rifles complete the equipment.

Near by the "Exchange," as it is now called, instead of "Canteen," shows its alluring sign. Here tobacco and beer are sold, and the soldiers amuse themselves when off duty in games of billiards and pool. Beyond the "Exchange" is the "Mess" quarters. On the long pine tables are large cups and plates, marked in large black letters "Q.M.D" "Quarter Master's Department." From the kitchen, in the rear, comes savory and mingled odors of coffee, meat, potatoes, and bread.

Farther down are the army tailors,' blacksmiths' and carpenters' shops . . . The guns have new quarters and opening from the great arched gallery are a series of rooms, given by the commandant for the use of the men.

By this time the two barbette-mounted Civil War-era rifled guns had been removed, and the empty Bastion A casemates were turned into enlisted recreation rooms which included a gym, theater stage and library.

A late 19th Century wooden guardhouse which once stood across from the Civil War guardhouse. It was in use from 1871-1890. The obsolete Civil War cannons are in the background ready to be scrapped during the Endicott Period.
National Archives

A photo of company barracks taken about 1915.
USS Salem Archives

Between 1890 and 1900 a mine casemate was constructed at Fort Warren. This was a small bombproof structure of poured concrete installed below ground within the Front IV curtain wall and across from Bastion D. It was built to detonate electrically controlled mines in the harbor. All of these improvements happened about the time of the brief Spanish-American War in 1898 and over the decade of 1892–1902.

On April 26, 1898, the 1st Regiment Massachusetts Heavy Artillery reported to Fort Warren to help out the regular artillery garrison.

The Endicott Period saw the construction of several other Boston Harbor coast defenses including Fort Banks and Fort Heath in Winthrop, Fort Andrews on Peddock's Island, Fort Revere in Hull, Fort Standish on Lovell's Island, and modifications to what became Fort Strong on Long Island. After World War I, Fort Duvall on Little Hog Island (now covered with condominiums and called "Spinnaker Island")was constructed. All of these forts together formed a formidable protective barrier around Boston Harbor. Although there were many test firings, none of these forts ever fired on hostile ships in either World War I or II.

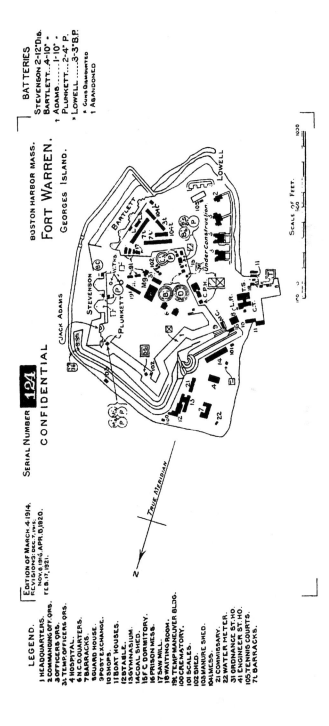

A 1921 military plan of Fort Warren, revised shortly after World War I, shows the buildings and concrete fortifications in existence at that time.
Coast Defense Study Group

World War I

In the winter of 1917–18 during World War I, reportedly about 1,600 men, including personnel from the 55th Artillery Coast Artillery Corps (C.A.C), were stationed at Fort Warren training for service overseas in Europe and defending the harbor. Just before World War I started, the fort was equipped with the following armaments:

> Two 4-inch Driggs-Schroeder Rapid Fire Guns mounted on pedestals in Battery Plunkett to cover the Narrows minefield.

> Four 10-inch Breech Loading Rifles (BLR) on disappearing carriages, mounted in Battery Bartlett, to cover the approaches to Boston.

> Two 12-inch Breech Loading Rifles (BLR) on disappearing carriages, mounted in Battery Stevenson, to cover the approaches to Boston.

> Three 3-inch Driggs-Seabury Rapid Fire Guns on balanced-pillar mounts in Battery Lowell to cover the Lighthouse Channel and Nantasket Roads minefield.

An early 20th century postcard of a 12-inch gun at Fort Monroe, Virginia. This is similar to the two guns once mounted in Battery Stevenson.
Author's Collection

*Non-commissioned Officers of the 10th Coastal Artillery Company,
Massachusetts Army National Guard. Photo taken at Fort Warren in
July 1915. Sgt. Frederick H. Lawton is standing at the far left.*
Photo courtesy of Paul Lawton, his grandson

The range of the most powerful of these guns was a huge
improvement over the Civil War armaments from roughly three
miles to over 9 miles. The newer large caliber guns had a loading
time to of 40–50 seconds. The projectiles had tremendous shock-
ing and explosive power compared to the previous ordnance.

The new disappearing gun emplacement located at Fort
Warren were designed not only to protect the crew, but more
importantly, to prevent the enemy from "zeroing-in" on the gun
itself—since it was hidden between firings. Hostile forces could
not tell exactly how many guns were in each battery either.

The guns were loaded in a sheltered position behind the
massive concrete emplacement walls and earth parapet. Heavy
counterweights raised the gun into its firing position above the
parapet by dropping into a well. The counterweights and the carriage system not only raised the gun but also cantilevered it forward so that it was above the parapet. When the gun was fired,
the recoil "disappeared" the gun back into its protective position for reloading.

The disappearing motion also brought the breech of the gun back to a convenient location for loading—no matter where the gun was aimed. This allowed these older weapons from the late 19th Century, which were loaded and operated entirely by hand, to fire as rapidly as WWII battleships that were loaded mechanically.

Nearly all of the Endicott Period concrete coast artillery gun emplacements on George's Island can still be seen today. Anything that is granite is the Civil War-era portion of the fort. Anything that is concrete is generally part of the pre-World War I Endicott Period seacoast fortifications.

By 1928, Fort Warren was deactivated and placed on caretaker status.

11

THE WORLD WAR II YEARS

In September 1940, Fort Warren was taken out of mothballs and designated as a Boston Harbor mine control operations support base. Telephone and radio communications were reactivated, and the army prepared the island for use as a training center for draftees. Fort Warren was an active U.S. Army fort throughout World War II. The fort played a prominent role in the defense of Boston Harbor against an anticipated German attack by U-boats or warships early in the war.

The Coast Artillery Corps of the U.S. Army was in charge of the care and service of fixed, railway, and tractor-drawn seacoast artillery, anti-aircraft artillery guns and machine guns. They also controlled submarine mines together with the fire control equipment, searchlights and related equipment.

In 1940, the 241st Coast Artillery (Harbor Defense) was assigned to Fort Warren. "We were there because of the possibility of an attack by sea or air. By the end of 1942 they started to transfer troops out, because there was no expected attack from the sea. They thought that submarines would shell Boston. There were supposedly German plans for an invasion of New England, but that never happened," said Edmund "Duke" MacNeil of Winthrop, Mass., a retired army captain who at that time was a sergeant stationed at Fort Warren during the winter of 1941–42.

"Training on the parade ground was equal to, and in remarkable coincidence, absolutely identical to a description of that activity written in a diary by a Civil War sergeant," said MacNeil who was in charge of training draftees. "At times I actually experienced a feeling of being on the parade ground back in 1862."

Surprisingly, there were only a few machine guns (.30 and .50 caliber) located at the fort for defense during World War II. The outdated, Spanish-American War-vintage 10- and 12-inch disappearing rifles were finally removed late in the war and sold for scrap after brief test firings and troop training in the early war years. Fort Warren's main WWII war defense contribution was anti-aircraft and vessel observation, artillery fire direction control and mine operations. Fort Warren was designated as a restricted military area with 24-hour guards on duty.

If an enemy ship happened to be sighted, the observers at the several forts (or stations associated with the forts) in the harbor would lock in the coordinates, communicate by telephone (or radio), to the appropriate plotting room which then directed the huge coast artillery guns to fire on the enemy vessel. "We had 5 meter radios and telephones, and ships would have been observed long before they got into range. Fort Banks was the headquarters and radio communication center. Fort Warren would do some firing and Fort Andrews on Peddock's Island would observe any ships coming in," said MacNeil.

Sgt. MacNeil was an expert observer and gunner. He also operated the Swayze Depression Position Finder that was located in Fort Warren's observation tower—which is still standing today on Bastion C. All the information went to a plotting room every three minutes. The plotters had to keep adjusting their calculations to account for the height of the tide so the shells wouldn't go over the ships. There were pre-WW II observation posts at Fort Andrews on Peddock's Island, Fort Standish on Lovell's Island, Nahant and Fort Revere in Hull. There were several other taller observation towers located along the northeast coast that were erected during the war.

In 1941, Fort Andrews fired of one of their 12-inch mortars at a towed target just outside of the harbor. The resulting blast reportedly forced one of the new barracks, standing directly behind he pit, two feet off its foundation, shattered all the windows and severed all the sewage pipes.

The navy operated vessels that opened up the submarine nets at the entrance to Boston Harbor to allow friendly ships to pass through. The submarine nets prevented the entry of any enemy surface torpedo boat or underwater craft. Outer Boston Harbor was also heavily mined. Boats operating out of Fort Warren actually laid and maintained the mines. The north minefield was electrically controlled by Fort Dawes—which was also the Harbor Entrance Command Post. Fort Dawes and the men stationed at Great Brewster Island also controlled the mines in Broad Sound.

Battery Stevenson firing the 12-inch disappearing rifle at a target in 1941. Gun #2 is firing, Gun #1 is in the foreground. Gun emplacements were numbered from right to left facing the enemy. It was reported that these guns were heard as far away as Milton.
Photo courtesy of Dorothy Snow Bicknell

Fort Warren controlled the Lighthouse Channel and Nantasket Roads minefield. Fort Dawes was equipped with a firing green and red light control panel for every mine in the harbor. Green signaled OK, red indicated when the mine when activated and fired.

Fort Warren's mine storage building and support structures had two railroad tracks going into it to service the mines before and after they were removed from the harbor. The Coast Artillery soldiers would clean the mines with steam and recharge them with fresh TNT.

According to MacNeil, after the mines were cleaned, the soldiers brought them outside with the tops removed. A couple of soldiers with buckets of TNT would hammer fresh TNT down (with a wooden tamper) into the mine until it had the prescribed amount, and then would seal it.

One day the army brought about 60–70 new draftees to the island for training and placed them into formation on the right hand side of the mine storage building. One draftee was observing the mine recharging procedure and asked, "What are those guys doing over there? Aren't those mines?"

"They're packing TNT into the mines," said one of the soldiers. The frightened trainees immediately took off and ran all over the island. It took hours to get them back recalled MacNeil.

There were two types of mines used in Boston Harbor during WWII: oval M2 buoyant mines which were anchored to the bottom and M4 ground mine systems. Both types could be fired by a controlled electrical charge, or turned into contact mines, and the M4 could also be set off by a magnetic field. They were anchored in ship channels and usually set for controlled firing.

The story of the Ghost of the Lady in Black was well known to the troops stationed at Fort Warren in World War II. When soldiers were assigned lonely guard duty on the parapets, they were often told, "Watch out for the Black Widow!"

Roy Markwith, a corporal with the 241st, was stationed at the fort briefly in early 1944. He, too, heard about the Ghost of the Lady in Black, but no one ever saw anything unusual during his duty at the fort

Although no enemy surface ships ever came near the fort, Fort Warren's soldiers were prepared. A huge 60 inch searchlight to protect the minefields was mounted in a concrete shelter just outside the walls on the seawall. It was left over from the Endicott period. Maintaining the searchlight was also one of the chores of the Coast Artillery soldiers stationed there.

Markwith's "Night Owls" searchlight insignia was one of the best known of his wartime creations. "The searchlights were a necessary aid for night activity," he said. "Each light put out one million candlepower." The searchlight crews lost a lot of sleep since their main duty was at night. They were constantly on night watch along the east coast especially after a German submarine landed spies on a New Jersey beach.

Life at the fort during World War II was not much different from life during the Civil War. Men slept in the same granite-walled rooms with small coal stoves for heat. Some NCOs lived underneath the sides along the sally port. Markwith remembers clearly, even after more than 50 years, the barracks in the casemates, "They were comfortable barracks, cool in the summer since they maintained the temperature."

Soldiers loaded up the pot belly stoves (called Cannon Heaters) with coal and got them cherry red in winter. "We used

Members of the U.S. Army's 241st Coast Artillery pose in front of the sally port in WWII.
USS Salem Archives

to put newspapers on our bunks, then the sheets on top, then two or three layers of newspapers. On top of that you put your blankets," said MacNeil who also slept in the room where Sawyer, the prisoner, made his escape from the demilune.

To keep the soldiers informed, the army printed and distributed a newspaper called *The Boston Harbor Defense Digest* which the soldiers in all of the forts, including Fort Warren, read to find out what was going on in the war and other news of the day.

Soldiers caught fish, lobsters and dug clams just as they did during the Civil War to supplement army rations. Fishing was good although they caught mostly sharks and skate. For a while the troops went pheasant hunting until the tall grasses were cut and the game disappeared. Battery F, 241st Coast Artillery used to bag a pheasant for their captain every Sunday. The original bakery was used for baking bread for a time, but it proved inadequate for their needs. It was turned into an NCO club where soldiers would play poker and other games for entertainment. Soldiers also played baseball, football and watched movies when off duty. The principal reliever of boredom was outwitting the Officer of the Day and sneaking off to the nearby town of Hull for weekend dances.

The Civil War guardhouse adjacent to the mine casemate, which can still be seen today, was used as a holding pen for unruly soldiers even in World War II. The old Civil War hospital was reportedly converted into a mess hall and later became a recreation facility.

Many of the coast artillerymen, who were stationed and trained at the forts in Boston, were sent south to train with field artillery units. These units were headed for Europe as the war had changed from defensive to offensive. The army realized that these soldiers already had extensive experience with powder and shells, so they were able to learn field artillery procedures quickly.

Under the Works Progress Administration (WPA) and Federal Arts Project, three artists were hired to paint murals in the Protestant Chapel at Fort Warren in 1940. The murals were to depict the writing of the song *John Brown*, the 6th Massachusetts Civil War Regiment marching off to Washington and the last meeting of the Union and Confederate Veterans that took place at Fort Warren in 1935. The artists began an exhaustive research into the uniforms of the Civil War to accurately depict the panel showing

Fort Warren's garrison taken in 1941. Battery Jack Adams is in the right center of the photo.
Photo by Raymond Hanson courtesy of Dorothy Snow Bicknell

the 6th Mass Regiment marching off to Washington. (They were shot at while passing through Baltimore. This was the cause of several of the Baltimore politicians being unwilling guests at Fort Warren.)

The artists borrowed a squad of WWII soldiers from Battery F, 241st Coast Artillery to model for the mural. These soldiers, as well as the rest of the battery, had previously posed for photos when Edward Rowe Snow had them marching and counter-marching until he got them in the same position on the parade ground as in an 1864 Civil War photograph.

Near the end of World War II, the enemy was no longer a threat from sea, and the army removed the last of Fort Warren's Spanish-American War-era armaments. Fort Warren lived out its final military days as an almost toothless, harbor mine control center. The heavy artillery was gone; all that remained were some anti-aircraft guns. The taxpayers got their money's worth from the fort. Fort Warren defended Boston from the beginning of the Civil War until the end of World War II.

The "John Brown" Chapel showing the murals on the walls. It was unfortunately destroyed by fire on May 16, 1981. More information about the chapel murals is in Appendix C.
Photo courtesy of Dorothy Snow Bicknell

By the early 1950s, the army removed all of the military equipment and placed the fort, for the very last time, into caretaker status. Vandals and looters quickly moved in and stripped the fort of all the marble mantel pieces, chandeliers and anything else they could find. Although caretakers were assigned until the state took possession in 1958, while the fort was under the General Services Administration (GSA) control, everything of any value was stolen.

Fort Warren sat silent and abandoned while the GSA tried to figure out what to do with it.

12

LEGENDS AND STORIES
(TRUE OR FALSE?)

Throughout the years, there have been many stories told about incidents at the fort. Most of them are probably true, but many of them are just that—great stories. Here is a collection of stories (some from the MDC archives). I suspect many of them were first recounted by Edward Rowe Snow, Gerald Butler or Al Schroeder. The sources were not named, but for the sake of telling the story of Fort Warren, here are some of the best stories.

The Hair and the Rat

The First Corps of Cadets was stationed at Fort Warren in May of 1862 during the Civil War. One day, one of the young men went into Boston for a haircut. The barber happened to use a sweet smelling oil on the cadet's hair. That night, the young cadet had strange dreams that he was being attacked by swarms of mosquitoes. The next morning he awoke and found all his well-oiled hair had been neatly clipped off by the resident rats at the fort. His hair reportedly never grew back.

The Attack of the Spanish Fleet

During the Spanish-American War, an observer watching the sea from Fort Warren saw four ships in a single file approaching the fort at night. He thought that the Spanish fleet was approaching. The lights, however, turned out to be a tug towing barges. The lights appeared to be blinking, and the soldier thought they were signals between enemy ships.

*The historic handshake between Union Veteran Charles Robinson (left)
and Confederate Veteran William B. Newell.*
Photo courtesy of Dorothy Snow Bicknell

The Last Meeting of the North and South

On June 9, 1935, while the fort was in caretaker status, patriotic
and historical societies dedicated a tablet to the famous southern prisoners who had been held at the prison. Confederate
Veteran William B. Newell shook hands with Union Veteran Charles
Robinson in front of the tablet. It was the last time Civil War veterans from both sides were together at the fort. An interesting
note according to historian Edward Rowe Snow concerned Union
veteran Robinson. As a small boy, Robinson had met and shaken
the hands of a 100-year old veteran of the Battle of Bunker Hill.
The old veteran's comrade was Dr. Joseph Warren who was killed
at the battle and for whom Fort Warren was named.

The Cannonball Incident

The cannonball story is one of the most popular stories about
the fort. When the fort was first built, the primary entrance was

through the sally port. About 1885, an opening was created in Bastion D so that people could get inside the fort without walking all the way around to the sally port. This opening, cut through a gun embrasure, became known as the new postern gate.

A private stationed at the fort in World War I decided to kill his captain for some unknown reason. He noticed that the captain had a set routine each evening. The captain would get off the boat, walk up to the new postern gate and enter the fort. The soldier climbed up above the portal with a 50-pound cannonball (left over from the Civil War) to drop onto his superior. The soldier thought he had it timed correctly, but the captain paused to light a cigarette. The soldier missed, and the cannonball smashed onto the

The crack in the slate walkway in Bastion D reportedly made by a cannonball.
Photo by Jay Schmidt

slate walkway. The round hole with cracks radiating from it can be clearly seen today. Two friends of the soldier reportedly dumped the cannonball into the cistern. The captain ordered a trial of the soldier, but without any evidence, there was no conviction.

In 1941, soldiers were cleaning out the cistern and found what was believed to be the cannonball used in the incident. They had heard Edward Rowe Snow tell the story about the cannonball incident a few years earlier. They presented the cannonball to him, but he was unable to take it home in his canoe at the time, and he had to leave it on the beach—where the tide unfortunately engulfed it. He had a standing offer of $50 for the lost cannonball, but no one could find it. In 1986 an MDC police officer discovered it and took it to the Mine Storage Building.

The Submarine and the Mine

During World War II, Boston Harbor was heavily mined. Fort Warren was one of the main mine control centers in the harbor. One night the officers in the mine casemate were alerted to a vessel coming near a contact mine in the minefield. German U-boats were known to patrol the east coast and there were no friendly submarines known to be in the area. The area was checked out by a patrol boat, but nothing was found. A light on the mine indicator panel suddenly went on.

At daylight when they recovered the mine, they found that it was full of water and had giant cuts in the side similar to those made by a propeller. There were traces of bronze on the cuts which would indicate it came from a German submarine. No one knows for sure what really caused the gash in the mine.

Gerald Butler says the story about the mine is true. There is a documented report about a U-boat operating near Fort Warren in WW II. Paul M. Lawton, a Naval and Maritime Historian, has researched the U-87, a 250-foot long, German Type VII diesel U-boat. The U-87 left its home base in France on May 19, 1942, with orders to attack allied ships off the New England coast.

On June 6, 1942, the U-87 was near Boston Light and secretly laying mines in the approaches to the Boston shipping lanes—not far from Fort Warren. The U-boat tripped a magnetic loop detection cable which set off signals at Point Allerton in Hull and Nahant.

According to Lawton, the U-87 quickly escaped before the U.S. Navy could react.

The next day, there was supposedly an underwater explosion in the submarine nets near Deer Island Light. The blast was felt in Boston and nearby Winthrop. (Back then there was strict censorship of any military-related news, and the newspapers would not have been allowed to publish this story.)

Sgt. Edmund "Duke" MacNeil, who had previously been stationed at Fort Warren, was on beach patrol at Fort Dawes on Deer Island a few weeks after the explosion in the nets. He found a life ring with Nazi markings that had washed up on the shore. Lawton said that it was the identical type of life ring that was mounted on Type VII U-boats and possibly came from the U-87 which had been prowling near Fort Warren and Boston Light.

Three Huckleberry Finns

Since Fort Warren is accessible only by boat, soldiers were isolated during their tours of duty on Georges Island. One June evening in 1941, three soldiers took the swimming raft, named "Mary Ellen" and attempted to float across Nantasket Roads to the nearby town of Hull where they hoped to attend a local Friday night dance. Unfortunately, the tide was going out to sea—and so did they. Some sailors at the U. S. maritime radioman school on Gallop's Island spotted them drifting past Great Brewster Spit. The Coast Guard rescued them in a small cutter and returned the three adventurers (and the raft) to the fort. They were given thirty days post restriction as punishment for the stunt.

The Battle of Bug Light

About ½ mile to the east of Fort Warren stood Bug Light which once marked the hidden sandbar that extends from Great Brewster Island towards the fort. The original lighthouse existed from 1856 until it burned in 1929. It was later replaced with an automated light on a small steel tower. The lighthouse was officially called the Narrows Lighthouse. The locals called it Bug Light because of the many iron stilts supporting the lighthouse made it look like a giant bug with long legs.

BUG LIGHT, BOSTON HARBOR, MASS.

An old postcard showing Bug Light which burned in 1929.
Author's Collection

During the Civil War, Fort Warren often went on alert whenever there were rumors of a possible Confederate Navy ship being sighted in the New England area. One rainy night, the sentries heard gunshots coming from the open sea. The shots continued, but no one could see anything in the downpour. The fort sent out an armed party in a small boat to investigate. When the boat returned, they explained the noise. The keeper of the nearby Bug Light was simply shooting rats with a shotgun. This incident was later jokingly referred to as, "The Battle of Bug Light."

Firing on the Nantasket Boat

Nantasket Beach is a popular ocean resort south of Boston and not too far from Fort Warren. About 1941 when the 241st Coast Artillery was stationed at the fort, they were engaging in target practice with the 12-inch guns of Battery Stevenson. About 4:45 P.M. a boat (believed to be the *Evangeline*) was hailed by a picket boat to prevent it from crossing into the target area where another boat was towing a target. The Nantasket boat refused to stop because they wanted to stay on schedule. The boat was about 600 yards from the fort and directly under the muzzle of the huge 12-inch gun.

The gun tube was loaded and very hot, and the officers were afraid it might cook off. The gun captain felt the vessel could not get near the blast; so he ordered the gun to fire. The big gun fired right over the boat—and it stopped dead in the water. Windows were blown out, crockery smashed, and people were running around in a panic. A soldier who witnessed the incident said, "It was like kicking an ant's nest." They watched and thought that many of the passengers were ready to jump overboard. The shot, by the way, landed very close to the target by Graves Light.

Demonstration Follies

One night in 1941 during a dance, some men of Battery F were showing their girlfriends the huge 12-inch disappearing guns in Battery Stevenson. A corporal was on one side explaining how the huge counterweight dropped and pulled the gun into the firing position. Meanwhile on the other side of the gun, a private decided to give an actual demonstration, and he raised the trip lever which dropped the weight. This caused the lever on the corporal's side to unexpectedly jump up and smash him in the nose. He was not amused.

New Technology Test

Shortly before World War II one of Fort Warren's sentries escorted a civilian and his strange equipment which he set up on Bastion B's parapet. This odd equipment (called a "cat's eye") was mounted on a tripod with a bipole antenna and was connected to the fort's electrical power. The man covered the equipment up with a black cloth, so the sentry could not see what was going on. The equipment was pointed towards the town of Hull and Boston Light. The technician was hidden under the cloth while a small boat went back and forth in front of the device.

The civilian said to himself, "It works," and started to write some notes with his back turned. The sentry quickly peeked under the cloth and observed "a green line on a lighted screen." The sentry had just witnessed an early radar test.

13

A NATIONAL HISTORIC LANDMARK

A fter World War II, Fort Warren still saw action as a mine service facility, finally being abandoned by the early 1950s—except for a caretaker. Historian Edward Rowe Snow, as president of the Society for the Preservation of Fort Warren, led the efforts to prevent this historical fort from becoming a repository for contaminated radiological materials. In the late 1950s because of the determination of many people, the General Services Administration (GSA) sold the fort and the property to the Commonwealth of Massachusetts.

The Metropolitan District Commission (MDC) officially took control on June 5, 1958. Fort Warren was not open to the public until 1961. Vandals, fires and the elements damaged many of the

The parade ground viewed in 1997 from Bastion A. Battery Stevenson's gun emplacements stand just to the right—outside of the photo.
Photo by Jay Schmidt

interior and exterior parts of the fort. All of the wooden and most of the brick buildings on the island used in both world wars had been destroyed by fires or razed.

In 1970, the fort and island were designated as the primary hub for a new Boston Harbor Islands State Park. Fort Warren was designated a National Historic Landmark also in 1970. Over the past 40 years more than 5 million people have visited the fort.

The first MDC curator, Gerald W. Butler, lived on the island on the top floor of the mine storage building in 1972 and 73. In 1975, the MDC wrote a contract for an archeological metal detector survey of certain areas of Fort Warren. The team used a variety of equipment, including an occasional bulldozer, and mapped out areas in large grids. Each area was photographed, and the team catalogued any items that they found in a detailed report.

This was the first time historians had been officially allowed to extract items from the grounds. The survey team searched several main areas including the parade ground, the Scarp Gallery, the ditch of Front III and part of the coverface.

In the parade ground, the survey team found a variety of items including iron plate door hinges, locks, bolts, mess equipment,

The powder magazine on the parade ground.
Photo by Jay Schmidt

brass cabinet hinges, dog tags, insignia, watches, keys, silverware, coins and rifle parts. They believed some of these items originated from 48 portable shacks erected in 1898 (to house the 1st Massachusetts Heavy Artillery) and later torn down.

The archeologists also found small arms ammunition, rifle and revolver casings and projectiles including a .58 caliber Minié ball used prominently in the Civil War.

On the parade ground just north of the Powder Magazine, they discovered horse, oxen and mule iron shoes. They also found a 6-inch pitching quoit (similar to a horseshoe pitching game) which had been mentioned previously by Confederate prisoners. As expected, the survey team also found buttons, badges, buckles and grommets. A large number of iron nuts, bolts and washers used on gun carriages were simply sheared off during dismantling and left on the ground.

Inside the casemates showing the huge, hammered granite blocks. The outside walls of the fort's casemates are six feet thick.
Photo by Jay Schmidt

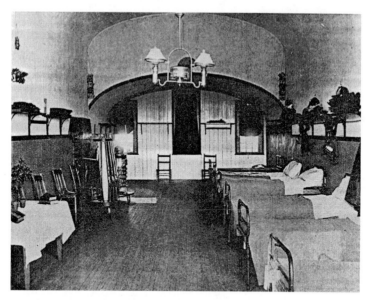

Soldier's living quarters in the casemates about 1893.
National Archives

*A similar casemate as it appeared in 1997. All of the wooden walls
and windows have been removed.*
Photo by Jay Schmidt

The team even found a huge heavy chain buried in the ground. According to Jim Fahey, the principal investigator, "We were unable to pull the chain out of the ground even using two MDC bulldozers. We believed it was a 'dead man' used to anchor block and tackle to raise and lower the granite blocks of the fort during construction or to move heavy ordnance." Also located in that area were many oxen shoes which gave further indication of heavy pulling.

The Boston Harbor Islands State Park—along with Fort Warren—became part of the National Park System in November 1996, by an act of Congress. The park includes roughly 30 islands and shoresites that are situated in Boston Harbor. This unusual park is managed by a 12-member Boston Harbor Islands Partnership comprised of representatives from various state and federal agencies. A 28-member Advisory Council makes recommendations to the Partnership about the development and implementation of the general plan for the islands. The Advisory Council is required to include representatives of municipalities, educational and cultural institutions, environmental organizations, business

This is Bastion C. The main observation and range tower constructed before World War I is on the left.
Photo by Jay Schmidt

and commercial entities including transportation, tourism and the maritime industry, advocacy organizations and Native American interests.

Although the legal name of the park is Boston Harbor Islands National Recreation Area, the park is known as Boston Harbor Islands, A National Park Area. This name was selected by the Boston Harbor Islands Partnership at the request of American Indians. They felt the word "recreation" was inappropriate and disrespectful to their ancestors who were imprisoned, died, and were buried on several of the islands. This name change allows the park to regard the islands as sacred ground. It centers the public's attention more on the park's natural resources and history rather than on its recreational aspects.

Each of the islands is currently managed by the agency or organization which owns the property (like the MDC at Fort Warren). The agencies work together, through the Partnership, however, to develop uniformity and to share in mutual programs.

The National Park Service also coordinates the Boston Harbor Islands Visitor's Center which is located at the Fan Pier in the Moakley Court House in South Boston. The Island Alliance, one of the partners, was formed in 1996, and provides financial support to the park and also plays a major role in the Visitor's Center.

──────────────────14

VISITING FORT WARREN

First opened to the public in 1961, Fort Warren continues as the centerpiece of the Boston Harbor Islands, A National Park Area. Although it is accessible only by water, nevertheless, the island hosts more than 100,000 visitors each summer. The island has floats for pleasure boats and a large pier for the harbor ferry boats which arrive several times a day from May through October. There are frequent daily seasonal boats to George's Island from Boston and Hingham.

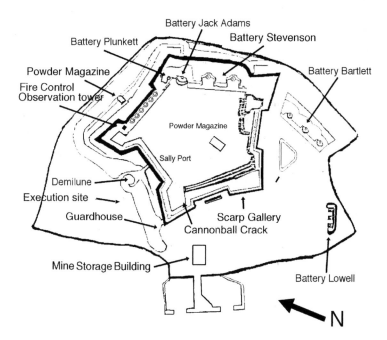

A visitor's map showing Fort Warren's key points of interest.
Illustration by Jay Schmidt based on an MDC map

The Mine Storage Building which is now the island's administration building and the first stop for visitors. The information area is outside to the left.
Photo by Jay Schmidt

The fort, however, can be viewed from the town of Hull. There is a small parking lot next to Hull High School where Fort Warren can be seen directly across Nantasket Roads.

If you plan to visit this historic fort, here are some suggestions.

Facilities

There are limited facilities on the island. Snacks are available at a small snack bar, but drinking water can be scarce. Bring your own water to be safe. There are many picnic tables and acres of grassy areas to spread a blanket and enjoy the view of Boston and nearby islands. Flush toilets and composting toilets are available. The MDC has installed signs around the fort identifying many interesting historical locations.

The Civil War guardhouse at the fort's entrance as it appeared in 1997.
Photo by Jay Schmidt

Key Points of Interest

This is a logical order in which to see these areas.

Mine Storage Building

The snack bar is located in the early 20th Century mine maintenance and repair building right next to the pier, and it is the starting point for any visit to the fort. Park rangers, assisted by the Friends of the Boston Harbor Islands, offer tours and will gladly answer questions. There is also an audiovisual show available.

Guardhouse

The main fort road, which leads to the sally port, is on the left of the fort and goes past the fort's original guardhouse which was in use during the Civil War. Visitors then pass under a concrete tunnel associated with the early 20th Century mine casemate which was added prior to WWI and is not part of the original fort.

Civil War Execution Site

The execution site where two deserters were shot during the Civil War is the flat area near the demilune. During that time there was an unbroken earth coverface in front of the fort which served as a backdrop for the bullets when the prisoners were shot. A portion of the Civil War-era earth coverface on the north flank of the demilune was later removed to allow military vehicles to enter through the sally port. The actual execution site was up against the coverface and believed to be on the right side of the demilune. The place where the garrison formed to watch the execution is now a picnic area.

Sawyer's Escape Musketry Loophole

The entrance to the fort's demilune (half-moon shaped fortification which protected the earthen coverface from an amphibious assault) is located across the ditch at one end of the sally port bridge outside of the fort. At the bottom left (facing the front of

The terreplein above Front II where the large 10-inch Rodman cannons were mounted towards the end of the Civil War.
Photo by Jay Schmidt

the demilune with the fort in the background) is the musket loophole where Sawyer escaped. The concrete patch that was placed in the hole that he chipped in the musketry loophole is plainly visible. During the Civil War, there was a ditch outside these walls, and he had to drop about 8–10 feet to the bottom.

Mason and Slidell Room

On the left (after walking through the sally port) is believed to be the famous room where Mason and Slidell were confined.

Fire Control Observation Tower and Rodman Cannon Mounts

Diagonally across the parade grounds up on the terreplein of Bastion C is the main observation and range tower used during WWI and WWII. The tower did not exist in the Civil War. A set of granite circular stairs leads up to it. You can also see where the large Rodman cannons were mounted on the ramparts. Their stone platforms and traverse stones are plainly visible on the terreplein next to the observation tower giving a sense of the type of the linear firepower in vogue during the mid 19th Century.

Battery Jack Adams

This single battery installed in Bastion B in the late 1890s was test fired, but later abandoned because of the poor quality of the concrete. It is a large semi-circular concrete battery visible from the parade ground opposite the sally port. This gun emplacement shows what Battery Bartlett looked like originally before the improvements in the early 20th Century were made.

Battery Stevenson

Directly across from the sally port up on the ramparts are two massive semi-circular concrete platforms for the huge 12-inch disappearing guns. These were installed just after the Spanish-American War and removed in the latter part of WWII.

The Scarp Gallery which is also called the Corridor of Dungeons.
Here is where the Lady in Black was supposedly captured.
Photo by Jay Schmidt

The Cannonball Crack

In front of the postern gate doorway (a rectangular opening on the right of a set of granite steps) in Bastion D is where the infamous cannonball reportedly crashed to the slate walkway when the soldier allegedly tried to kill his superior officer. It is still clearly visible.

The Corridor of Dungeons

On the outer scarp wall of Bastion E, facing the pier is a large, granite-walled section originally designed to hold soldiers with muskets to fire on any troops who landed and attempted to take the fort. This section has many vertical musket loopholes. Technically called a Scarp Gallery, this is the area of the fort where the Lady in Black was supposedly captured. Her ghost has been seen in this area. Visitors have to go up a wooden staircase and crawl through a flank howitzer embrasure and over the remains of the fort's second 1890s mine casemate to get inside.

Battery Bartlett

Outside the walls of the fort, on the fort's old ravelin earthworks, sits Battery Bartlett which mounted four 10-inch disappearing guns during both world wars. The battery is presently cordoned off (and off-limits) because of the decaying condition. In the 1970s the seawall in front of the battery needed repair, and the number 4 gun emplacement was demolished, and the rubble was used to help repair the area. There are only three gun positions remaining.

Battery Lowell

Also outside the fort's walls, on the south shore of the island, is Battery Lowell which once had three 3-inch Driggs-Seabury Rapid Fire Guns on balanced-pillar mounts. This battery was constructed in 1899 to cover the Lighthouse Channel mine field and abandoned shortly after World War I.

Fort Warren as it appears today. Photo taken December 29, 1999.
Photo by Ryan Vines

What to Bring

Besides drinking water and a light snack, bring a camera, jacket, comfortable walking shoes, sunblock and a flashlight. Many of the areas are poorly illuminated and a flashlight will help you to explore these areas. Binoculars are also handy to observe passing ships and nearby islands.

When walking around the fort, keep to formal pathways or lawns, and stay out of overgrown areas. It was built as a fortification so there can be sudden drops. Please respect fences and warnings signs.

_____ Appendix A

FORT WARREN'S
BATTERY DATA

Coast artillery batteries were usually named after officers or war heroes. Once a battery was named, the name was almost never changed. Gun emplacements were numbered from right to left—facing the enemy.

Battery Bartlett

Named for: Brevet Maj. Gen. William F. Bartlett, former Colonel 49th & 57th Regiments Massachusetts Volunteer Infantry.
Built: 1892–98
Type: Four 10-inch M-1888 rifles on M-1894 and M-1896 disappearing carriages.
Maximum range: 14,201 yards with a 617 lb. long-point projectile.
Modifications: Loading platforms widened, new rooms added at the rear, concrete wall separating two small interior rooms was removed and new free-standing brick room built to protect powder from moisture. Guns removed in 1918 and rearmed about 1920. Hoists widened for long-point shells.

By the 1970s, the seawall by Bastion A collapsed and only twenty feet of land was left in front of the fort wall. The area was repaired at a cost of $776,000. To accomplish this, gun emplacement #4 was removed. Only three gun emplacements remain.
Disarmed: 1943

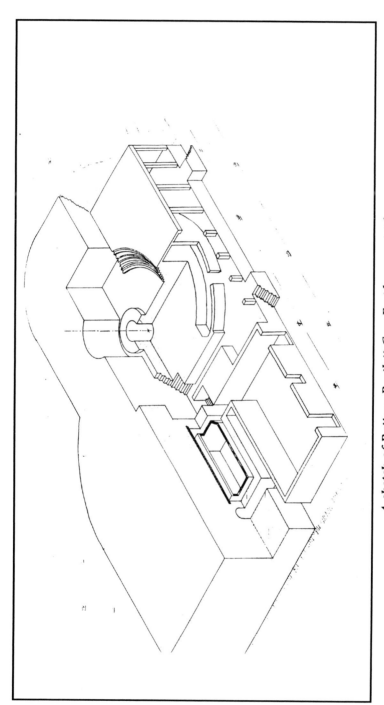

A sketch of Battery Bartlett Gun Emplacement #1.
Illustration by Tom Vaughan

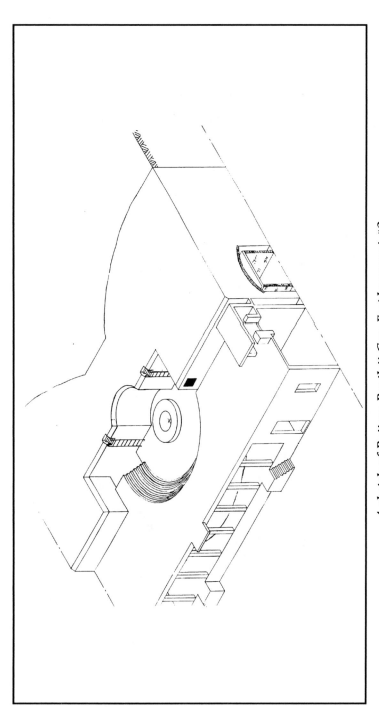

A sketch of Battery Bartlett Gun Emplacement #2.
Illustration by Tom Vaughan

Battery Bartlett showing three of its four 10-inch guns. These three gun emplacements remain today. Gun emplacement #4 is out of the photo at the far left. It was demolished in the 1970s. Photo taken about 1941.

Photo courtesy of Dorothy Snow Bicknell

Battery Jack Adams

Named for: Capt. John G. B. Adams, 19th Massachusetts Volunteer Infantry. Wounded at Gettysburg, Medal of Honor winner.
Built: 1892–98
Type: One 10-inch M-1888 rifle on M-1894 disappearing carriage.
Maximum range: 14,201 yards with a 617 lb long-point projectile.
Modifications: An experimental construction using weak Rosedale concrete and abandoned in mid 1910s.
Disarmed: about 1914

Battery Lowell

Named for: Brig. Gen. Charles Russell Lowell, former Colonel 2nd Massachusetts Cavalry. Mortally wounded at Cedar Creek, Virginia.
Built: 1899–1900
Type: Three 3-inch Rapid Fire Driggs-Seabury M-1898 guns on M-1898 balanced-pillar mounts.
Modifications: Balanced-pillar mounts were fixed in upper position in 1916.
Disarmed: about 1920

Battery Plunkett

Named for: Sgt. Thomas Plunkett, 21st Massachusetts Volunteer Infantry. Lost both arms at Fredericksburg, Virginia.
Built: 1898
Type: Two 4-inch Rapid Fire Driggs-Schroeder M-1896 guns on M-1896 pedestal mounts.
Modifications: None
Disarmed: about 1925

Battery Stevenson

Named for: Brig. Gen. Thomas G. Stevenson, First Colonel 24th Massachusetts Volunteer Infantry. Killed in action at Spotsylvania, Virginia.

Built: 1899–1902

Type: Two 12-inch M-1895 rifles on M-1897 disappearing carriages.

Maximum range: 27,600 yards with a 1,070 lb long-point projectile.

Modifications: New free-standing brick powder rooms, new Taylor-Raymond shell hoists for long point shells. The magazines and shell rooms were within the old granite casemates with shafts cut through the roof for shell hoists. Maximum elevation increased for longer range.

Disarmed: 1944

Source: Conference Notes for the 6th Annual Conference of the Coast Defense Study Group. *The Harbor Defenses of Boston.* August 1988. Revised by Tom Vaughan. Additional data provided by Bill Stokinger.

Battery Stevenson's 12-inch Gun #1 in the firing position. Photo taken about 1941.
Photo courtesy of Dorothy Snow Bicknell

Battery Stevenson's 12-inch Gun #2 in the firing position. Note the 2 painted on the wall. Gun emplacements were numbered from right to left—facing the enemy. Photo taken about 1941.
Photo courtesy of Dorothy Snow Bicknell

The huge 12-inch Gun #2 of Battery Stevenson fires at a target. Gun #1 (in the foreground) is being loaded in the recoiled position. Photo taken about 1941.

Photo courtesy of Dorothy Snow Bicknell

Battery Stevenson's Gun #2 firing at a target. The blasts could be felt at the hospital in Quincy when these big guns were engaged in target practice. Photo taken about 1941.
Photo courtesy of Dorothy Snow Bicknell

—————— Appendix B

FOR MORE
HISTORIC INFORMATION
ABOUT FORT WARREN

Metropolitan District Commission
Reservations and Historic Sites Division
20 Somerset St.
Boston, MA 02108

Other Sources

Boston Athenaeum
10½ Beacon St.
Boston, MA 02108

Boston Harbor Islands
A National Park Area
408 Atlantic Ave., Suite 228
Boston, MA 02110-3350

The Bostonian Society
Old State House
206 Washington Street
Boston, MA 02109-1713

Coast Defense Study Group, Inc.
1560 Somerville Rd.
Bel Air, MD 21015

The Hull Lifesaving Museum, Inc.
1117 Nantasket Ave.
Hull, MA 02045

Library of Congress
Prints and Photographs Division
Washington, DC 20540

Massachusetts Historical Society
154 Boylston St.
Boston, MA 02215

National Archives and Records Administration
700 Pennsylvania Ave.
Washington, DC 20408

National Archives and Records Administration
860 Adelphi Rd.
College Park, MD 20740-6001

National Archives–New England Region
380 Trapelo Rd.
Waltham, MA 02154

U.S. Army Military History Institute (USAMHI)
22 Ashburn Drive
Carlisle, PA 17013-5008
ATTN: Inquiries

USS Salem Archives Museum
U.S. Naval Ship Building Museum
P.O. Box 66
N. Quincy, MA 02171

_____Appendix C

THE JOHN BROWN
CHAPEL MURALS

The so-called "John Brown"Chapel was destroyed by fire on May 16, 1981. It had colorful murals painted on the walls of the Protestant Chapel during World War II. It was located in a casemate next to the sally port.

This wall depicts the writing of the John Brown Song. The spirit of John Brown, the abolitionist, hovers above the soldier writing the lyrics. The soldiers of the 12th Massachusetts are singing the song on the right.
Photo courtesy of Dorothy Snow Bicknell

This panel shows the 6th Massachusetts Regiment marching off to war from Fort Warren. They were later fired upon in Baltimore.
Photo courtesy of Dorothy Snow Bicknell

The last meeting of the veterans of the North and South at Fort Warren on June 9, 1935 is depicted here.
Photo courtesy of Dorothy Snow Bicknell

Union veterans after the war are shown in the last panel.
Photo courtesy of Dorothy Snow Bicknell

Historian Edward Rowe Snow with his movie camera in front of the smoldering chapel shortly after the fire was put out.
Photo by Al Schroeder courtesy of Dorothy Snow Bicknell

MDC Historian and Photographer Al Schroeder, Edward Rowe Snow and his wife Anna-Myrle Snow, stand in front of the still-smoking chapel. It was said that the famed historian Edward Rowe Snow had tears in his eyes when he saw that the murals had been destroyed.
Photo courtesy of Dorothy Snow Bicknell

Glossary

Bastion – The arrowhead-shaped, projecting part of a fort appended to where two fronts join. They were designed to provide perpendicular flanking firepower along the walls if needed.

Barbette – Also called "en barbette." A method of mounting artillery to fire over a parapet.

BLR – Breech-Loading Rifle. Where the projectile is inserted from the rear of a rifled weapon.

Casemate – An interior room of a fort usually one from which guns are fired through openings called embrasures.

Cistern – A tank for holding rainwater or well water.

Cook off - When a loaded gun fires unexpectedly because of a hot barrel or other unusual circumstances.

Coverface – An earthwork, offset from the fort's scarp walls to protect the fort's masonry from artillery shells.

Demilune – A curved, fortified outerwork of a fort. (It is French for half-moon.) Fort Warren's demilune is located on the coverface just outside of the fort at the foot of the sally port bridge. Rarely spelled with the hyphen "demi-lune."

Depression Ranger Finder – An instrument developed in the late 1800s to aim artillery by calculating range and bearing data from one position.

Ditch – A trench around a fort to help protect it from foot soldier attack.

Front – The sides of a fort usually defined from the salient tip of one bastion to the salient tip of another bastion. Generally corresponds to the parade curtain wall.

139

Magazine – A place where explosive propellant or powder is kept safely.

MDC – Metropolitan District Commission. The Massachusetts government agency responsible for the administration and maintenance of Fort Warren.

MLR – Muzzle-Loading Rifle. Where the projectile is inserted down the mouth/muzzle of a rifled weapon.

Parade ground – A large open area used by the troops for drilling, marching and recreation. Usually refers to the main space encompassed by the walls of a fortification.

Parapet – A protective wall, or elevation of earth or stone, that protects soldiers and artillery.

Rampart – A broad embankment or structure raised as a fortification and usually surmounted by a parapet.

Rodman – A type of Civil War-era smooth-bore cast iron cannon invented by Thomas J. Rodman, a U.S. Army ordnance officer.

RF – Rapid fire. A class of artillery using fixed ammunition which allowed for quick reloading and firing.

Sally port – An entrance or portal into a fort. Used to exit the fort quickly to attack enemy soldiers if needed.

Scarp Gallery – A series of casemates along a fort's outer scarp wall from which artillery fires through embrasures or small arms fires through musketry loops.

Sutler – Merchants who followed Civil War units to sell items to the soldiers.

Terreplein – The level space behind a parapet or rampart where guns are mounted.

Bibliography

Avary, Myra Lockett, ed. *The Recollections of Alexander H. Stephens. His diary kept as a prisoner at Fort Warren 1865.* Baton Rouge: Louisiana State University Press, 1998.

Boston *Herald.* March 23, 1864 page 4.

Boston *Herald.* April 23, 1864 page 2.

Catton, Bruce. *The American Heritage New History of the Civil War.* New York: Viking, 1996.

Denney, Robert E. *Civil War Prisons & Escapes.* New York: Sterling

Garrison, Webb. *Creative Minds in Desperate Times.* Nashville: Rutledge Hill Press., 1997.

Harper's Weekly, "Fort Warren, Boston," Sat. Dec. 7, 1861, Vol. V No. 258, NY.

Hesseltine, William B. *Civil War Prisons.* Ohio: Kent State University Press, 1972.

Howard, F. K. *Fourteen Months in American Bastilles.* Baltimore: Kelly, Hedian & Piet. 1863.

Jenkins, James Beale H. "The Author of the John Brown Song." *The Magazine of History,* June 1910.

McLain, Minor H. *Prison Conditions in Fort Warren, Boston, During the Civil War.* Boston University, Mugar Library: PhD dissertation, 1955.

Metropolitan District Commission. *George's Island Study Guide* and various materials compiled by Al Schroeder, Boston.

Parkman, Aubrey. *Army Engineers In New England.* Waltham, MA, 1978.

Pictorial War Record. Sat. Apr. 8, 1882. p. 255-256. NY.

Sangston, Lawrence. *The Bastiles [sic] of the North.* Baltimore: Kelly, Hedian & Piet, 1863.

Sarty, Roger F. *Coast Artillery 1815-1914.* Alexandria Bay, NY: Museum Restoration Service Publication, 1988.

Shurcliff & Merrill. *History and Master Plan George's Island and Fort Warren.* Boston: Metropolitan District Commission, 1960.

Snow, Edward Rowe. *An Island Citadel.* Boston: Glenrose Press.

Snow, Edward Rowe. *Historic Fort Warren.* Boston: The Yankee Publishing Company, 1941.

Snow, Edward Rowe. *The Romance of Boston Bay.* Boston: The Yankee Publishing Company, 1946.

Sweetser, M.F. *King's Handbook of Boston Harbor.* (Reprint.) Friends of the Boston Harbor Islands, Inc. Publication.

"The John Brown Song." *The Bivouac,* Jan. 1885.

The Harbor Defenses of Boston. Conference Notes. Maryland: Coast Defense Study Group Press, 1988.

Index

About the Author – Jay Schmidt

 Jay, a 10th generation New Englander, is the great-great grandson of a Union soldier. During the research for this book, he discovered that his great grandmother's uncle was a soldier in the 12th Massachusetts Regiment who most likely sang the *John Brown* song while he was "mustered in" at Fort Warren.

His grandfather, Charlie Schmidt, was the creator of *Sgt. Pat of Radio Patrol*, a police comic strip which was nationally syndicated in the 1930s and 40s. His father, Jim Schmidt, a retired newspaper artist, contributed some of the illustrations in this book.

Jay is a Civil War reenactor, and he is a member of the New England Department of the Council on America's Military Past. During the Vietnam War, he served in the U.S. Coast Guard as a radioman. He is a former Vermont State Game Warden, and he is currently a publishing manager in Boston.

Jay has published many magazine articles as a writer and photographer. His articles have appeared in *Yankee, New England Printer & Publisher, Vermont Life* and other periodicals. He holds a master's degree in Mass Communication from Boston University. Jay lives in Norton, Massachusetts, with his wife Donna. They have two grown children, Jennifer and Jeff.

http://jay.schmidt.home.att.net/ft.warren

COAST DEFENSE
STUDY GROUP

DEDICATED TO THE STUDY OF SEACOAST FORTIFICATIONS

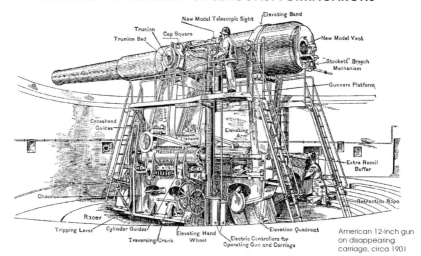

American 12-inch gun on disappearing carriage, circa 1901

CDSG Membership Benefits:

- The Quarterly Coast Defense Journal
- The Quarterly CDSG Newsletter
- Annual Conferences held at fortification sites around the United States
- Special tours to fortification sites around the world

The Coast Defense Study Group
634 Silver Dawn Ct.
Zionsville, IN 46077-9088

WWW.CDSG.ORG